Chicago Mountain Bike Trails Guide

A dirt-lover's escort to the best off-road bicycle trails in northeastern Illinois and beyond...

Chicago Mountain Bike Trails Guide

by P.L. Strazz

Third Edition

Big Lauter Tun Books
Chicago

Created, written and designed by P.L. Strazz

Cover art by Jay Riley

All photos by Strazz except as noted below:
Pgs. 31, 44, 76, 98 by Dean Rinaldi
Pg. 83 by Debra Strazzabosco
Pg. 101 by Daniel Brady

Front and back cover photos taken at Crystal Ridge Ski Hill.

Direct any questions or comments to:

Big Lauter Tun Books
P.O. Box 25094
Chicago, IL 60625
bltbooks.com
orders@bltbooks.com

ISBN: 0-9646310-6-7

CONTENTS

Northeastern Illinois

CONTENTS continued...

Southern Wisconsin

Northern Indiana

Southwestern Michigan

For Isabel and Leo

WARNING:
Big Lauter Tun Books
will not be responsible
for injuries, accidents
or fines incurred by
people exploring trails
featured in this book.
Ride safely, respect
other users and obey
all trail policies.

INTRODUCTION

It's no minor achievement when a book manages to incorporate the words "Chicago" and "Mountain" in its title, but it's happened for the third time with this latest edition of "Chicago Mountain Bike Trails Guide."

Much has happened since the previous two editions tuned riders in to the Chicago area's best off-road trails, first in 1995 and then again in 1998. Policies have changed, some trails have closed and others have been built. Overall, off-road bicycling opportunities are as expansive as ever and, if you don't mind traveling up to an hour or two before you ride, this book will keep you busy for a long time.

More than 15 riding locations were added to the third edition, along with maps and photos, making the book the most comprehensive database ever published on Chicago area mountain bike trails. Only trails with natural tread surfaces are profiled; no paved ones are included unless they provide access to another path that's appropriate for fat tires. If you're looking for paved trails, you've got the wrong book.

Why is it important to know where the best trails are? Because enjoyment of the sport hinges on factors like a trail's difficulty, length, scenery and proximity to home. And no matter how thrilling it can be to ride a favorite trail time and again, there's nothing like experiencing a new and exciting path, riding through forests you've never seen before and wondering what lies over the next hill. Finding out is even better.

When exploring trails featured here, pay attention to any regulations that may have been implemented that restrict bicycles. While every profiled trail was legal for riding at time of publication, it doesn't mean they always will be.

If you have never ridden off-road (industry sources estimate 80 percent of mountain bike purchasers never do), try the easy trails first and go from there.

Preserve the trails for the enjoyment of other users by riding responsibly. Refer to the rear of this book and read the International Mountain Biking Association's trail rules and adhere to them at all times. And to preserve the old noggin', always wear a helmet.

How to use this book

Each trail profiled in the guide includes at least two maps, an in-depth description, photos and reference chart. The maps are of two varieties: One indicates the location of a trail in relation to major Chicago-area highways, and the other shows the actual trail route, parking areas, natural landmarks, and other useful information. Not all maps are to scale. Symbols are defined at right. For bicycling areas that have a paved trail in addition to dirt trails, surfaces are also indicated in writing. The reference chart is explained below:

Physical Challenge: Stars are used to indicate a riding area's physical challenge due to elevation changes. Four stars mean an area has a lot of large hills, while one star means the area is nearly flat. Trails in the guide are rated in comparison to each other, so a four-star northeastern Illinois trail is not equivalent to a four-star Rocky Mountain trail.

Technical Challenge: Stars are used to indicate an area's technical challenge due to obstacles such as fallen logs, ruts, rocks and turns. Four stars mean the area has a lot of obstacles, while one star means there are few.

Singletrack: A percentage is used to indicate how much of a trail system is comprised of a single, thin path. This category assumes that singletrack is the most sought after type of trail.

Doubletrack: A percentage is used to indicate how much of a trail system is comprised of two thin, parallel trails, or unpaved roads.

Length: Indicates miles of trail.

Distance from Loop: Indicates how far a bicycling location is in miles from downtown Chicago.

Tread: Indicates the surface of a trail. Non-natural surfaces such as asphalt and pavement are only listed if a rider has to use such a section to get to another section with a natural surface.

NORTHEASTERN ILLINOIS

PART I

Veteran Acres
Park

(815) 459-0680

Physical Challenge:	☆ ☆
Technical Challenge:	☆
Singletrack:	40 %
Doubletrack:	50 %
Length:	4+ miles
Distance from Loop:	50 miles
Tread:	dirt, grass

Compared to county forest preserves and state recreation areas, city parks don't have much of a reputation for off-road bicycling. But Veteran Acres Park in suburban Crystal Lake is a 150-acre exception to the rule. With an idyllic mixture of hills, prairies and woodlands connected by rolling multipurpose paths, the park is scenic as it is challenging. Climbs and de-

scents of 50 feet or more are not uncommon here, and the views alone make for an enjoyable ride.

Named for soldiers returning from World War II, Veteran Acres was a golf course before the city acquired it in 1928 and gradually restored it to its natural condition. Because its trails were laid for hiking and have only recently been used by mountain bikers, distance-wise they are short. Sections frequently intersect each other, but because they are so much fun, it seems hardly redundant to ride the same trail twice.

The trails are maintained by the Crystal Lake Park District and their width varies between four and six feet. The tread is

grass, cut short with a lawnmower, and a thin strip of dirt runs down the center.

The longest uninterrupted trail in the park runs for about a mile beneath a set of Commonwealth Edison power lines. Mostly gravel, the trail is as hilly as those in the rest of the park, but not nearly as scenic.

In the mid-1980s, the park district acquired a 120-acre forest attached to Veteran Acres called Sterne's Woods. Together, the two parcels bear more than a striking resemblance to the Kettle Moraine State Forest in southern Wisconsin. Both are located on the same 100-mile-long moraine, and both are popular with bikers in search of hills.

The area's newfound popularity did not come without consequences. Trail signs were erected to prohibit bikes and horses

in Sterne's Woods' most sensitive areas, restricting them to a 3-mile gravel path which circles its perimeter. The park district also implemented an education campaign that has uniformed police patrolling the area on all-terrain vehicles and bicycles.

Despite numerous trail closures in Sterne's Woods, its main path is as challenging as the grass trails next door in Veteran Acres.

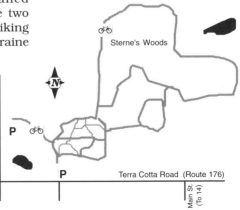

Chain O'Lakes
State Park

(847) 587-5512

Physical Challenge:

Technical Challenge:

Singletrack: - %

Doubletrack: 5 %

Length: 6 miles

Distance from Loop: 65 miles

Tread: crushed limestone

For Chicago-area bicyclists who have never been to Chain O'Lakes State Park, learning that it has an off-road bicycle trail can come as some surprise. After all, how can the heart of Illinois' largest concentration of natural lakes have room for a trail with three separate loops and a couple of mile-long extensions? Isn't there just too much darn water around?

Not exactly. The park isn't nearly as water oriented as its name portends to be. In fact, the park doesn't even have a beach. Virtually all of its 6,000 acres are on good old terra firma, and nary a half mile of the bike trail comes within eyeshot of water.

Most of the trail weaves through huge expanses of woods and marsh and, like the five other northeastern Illinois state parks that have groomed off-road bicycle trails, the tread is crushed limestone. It runs about eight feet wide and is designed to be as accessible as possible,

which makes it perfect for novice riders. Experts, forget it, unless you really appreciate scenery or like to explore new places.

All of the park's picnic areas are connected to the trail system. Each route is marked with some very explicit signs, such as poles that mark every one-tenth of a mile, and maps at every intersection. Other signs, such as ones that indicate hills with the image of a bike at a 45-degree angle, are a bit dramatic, but a nice touch, anyway.

Since the bulk of the trail system was built in the early 1990s, visitors to the park have been on the upswing. About 1.5 million people visit annually, a healthy chunk with bikes in tow.

Gold Finch Trail is arguably the most scenic of the loops because part of it runs along the Fox River. The loop also has a few moderate hills that offer knockout views of McHenry County and one of the only stretches of doubletrack in the park.

The doubletrack isn't long, just a half-mile, but its grass and dirt surface is a nice relief from the crushed limestone. The only singletrack in the park is on horse trails, which are off limits to bikes.

Badger and Sunset trails are also very scenic. Both weave in and around towering oaks and cottonwoods, and along the edges of prairies and marshes. A mile-long trail that is connected to Sunset is pretty much more of the same. A bridge crossing on Sunset is the technical highlight.

Because each loop in Chain O'Lakes is less than 2 miles, it's not really a place where you can spend all afternoon covering new ground. A lot of visitors are families who spend the day picnicking and going on short joy rides.

The park was named Chain O'Lakes because three lakes form part of its eastern bor-

der. The park is also bordered by the Fox, which connects seven of 10 lakes in the chain.

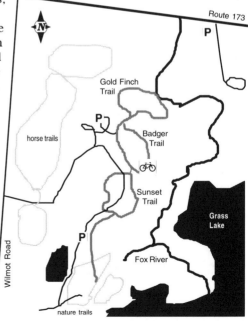

DesPlaines River
Trail
(847) 367-6640

Physical Challenge: ✮ ✩
Technical Challenge: ✩
Singletrack: 10 %
Doubletrack: 10 %
Length: 18 miles
Distance from Loop: 35 miles
Tread: limestone screenings,
            wood chips, dirt

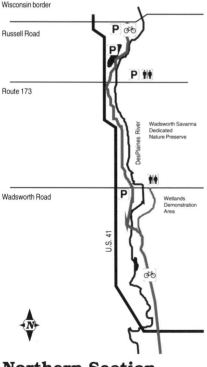

Northern Section

While there are many places to ride along the DesPlaines River in northeastern Illinois, only two stretches of trail in Lake County are actually named after the river. They're each about 9 miles and have a variety of other users besides mountain bikers, including hikers, joggers, and equestrians. In snow months they're also used by cross-country skiers and snowmobilers.

Both northern and southern sections of the DesPlaines River Trail are made of crushed limestone and run through the DesPlaines River Valley. Elevation changes are moderate and, in many areas, nonexistent.

The northern section of the DesPlaines River Trail runs between a portion of U.S. Highway 41 on the south and Russell Road on the north. The bike route cuts through open grasslands and two forest preserves: the 972-acre Van Patten Woods and 1,200-acre Wadsworth

Savanna. Each has its own wood chip trails.

The river valley is wider in the northern section than in the southern section. In the Wetlands Demonstration Project, it forms several wetland basins that provide a rich habitat for wildlife. Nice views all around.

The southern section is closer to Chicago and stretches between Half Day Road on the south and Route 176 on the north. The section is dotted with four preserves: the 329-acre Old School Forest, 504-acre MacArthur Woods, 327-acre Wright Woods and 201-acre Half Day Forest. Inside each are unmapped trails made of dirt and wood chips.

The Forest Preserve District plans on eventually connecting the northern and southern sections and, when it does, it will be possible to ride along the DesPlaines River from Madison Street in Cook County to the Wisconsin border.

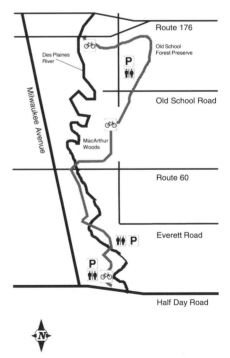

Southern Section

Gander Mountain
Forest Preserve
(847) 367-6640

Physical Challenge: ☆☆☆
Technical Challenge: ☆☆
Singletrack: 15 %
Doubletrack: 80 %
Length: 4+ miles
Distance from Loop: 60 miles
Tread: dirt, gravel

Gander Mountain Forest Preserve is one of the most interesting bicycling locations in the Chicago area. Bordering the Wisconsin state line in northwestern Lake County, the preserve is home to the highest point in Lake County, hence the name, but the county Forest Preserve District doesn't do much to hype the area. It has no parking lot, no paved roads, and no signed trails. A single Gander Mountain Forest Preserve sign on the east side of Wilmot Road is all there is to find the place. An abandoned grain silo works equally well. Park at the turnoff on the side of the road.

Leading from the road, a gravel path heads south, then east, into wooded, interior areas of the preserve. The path is the only route leading inside, but don't worry about missing it because it's easy to see. Cruise on it for a half mile until it enters the trees and forks in two directions.

Either route from the fork makes

for a twisty ride. The right side of the fork is doubletrack and gradually descends through trees for about a half mile before coming to a dead end at a private farm. There's a path that reportedly leads all the way to the Fox River from near this spot, but it can be tough to find for new visitors. Best to head back on the developed trail.

The path to the left of the fork narrows and climbs a steep, winding incline to the top of Lake County's highest peak, 957 feet above sea level. An innocuos survey pole marks the spot. The view is tremendous: Chain O'Lakes State Park and Grass Lake are visible to the southeast, and to the west, the farmland of northern Illinois. To the north is Gander Mountain ski area, which shares the same hill, but on the Wisconsin side of the border.

There are a couple of long, narrow trails that stretch from the top of Gander Mountain all the way to the base, but they veer off of public property and are not open to bicycling.

County bicycling polices instruct riders to stay on the preserve's developed paths.

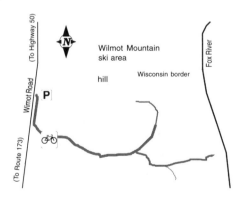

Rock Cut
State Park
(815) 885-3311

Physical Challenge:	☆ ☆ ☆
Technical Challenge:	☆ ☆
Singletrack:	30 %
Doubletrack:	60 %
Length:	10+ miles
Distance from Loop:	85 miles
Tread:	dirt, sand

Unlike some other northeastern Illinois state parks and forest preserve districts that try to discourage mountain biking, Rock Cut State Park openly promotes it. It has 10 miles of off-road trails that form a couple of different loops around the park.

One of the loops is the 4.25-mile Main Trail, which runs around scenic Pierce Lake. The route is dirt and cuts through the park's wooded areas and tackles several small hills. It's about eight feet wide to accommodate cross-country skiers. The Main Trail also has several sub-loops that can make for longer or shorter rides.

Another loop snakes around the northeast corner of the park.

Like the main loop, it leads through dense trees, is hilly and well marked. Parts run through open meadows and native prairie grasses. Special trail signs inform riders where to go and which trail they're on.

There is also a 14-mile horse and snowmobile trail as well as several unmapped miles of singletrack.

To find some of the thinnest trails, start from the closest parking lot to Lone Rock in the southwest section of the park. From there, descend into a shallow valley and look for Willow Creek. A small maze of thin, dirt trails are located on both sides of the creek.

The earliest known users of the land were Miami Indians in the

mid-1600s. Later, the Winnebago, then the Fox and Sauk settled here. After 1800, it was Potawatomi, Ottawa and Chippewa territory, but they ceded it to the federal government after the Black Hawk War, according to the Illinois Department of Natural Resources.

Rock Cut State Park opened in 1955 and has since become popular for a variety of activities. In addition to the expansive trail system, fishing, boating, swimming and camping are popular.

The park was named in honor of railroad workers who laid tracks through the area more than 100 years ago. Because the terrain here is so rocky, they had to do a lot of cutting -- hence the name. The railroad tracks were removed when Pierce Lake was dammed and enlarged.

With 3,092 acres, there are challenges for mountain bikers of all skill levels.

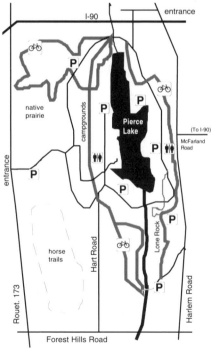

Kickapoo
State Park
(217) 442-4915

Physical Challenge:	☆ ☆
Technical Challenge:	☆ ☆
Singletrack:	85 %
Doubletrack:	10 %
Length:	12 miles
Distance from Loop:	170 miles
Tread:	dirt, gravel

The view from I-74 in Downstate Illinois doesn't reveal much about mountain biking in the bread basket of the Prairie State. All you see are acres of farms, a flat horizon and an occasional patch of trees. Turn on the car radio and you hear a medley of hits dating from 20 years ago.

Despite the lackluster drive, Kickapoo State Park is a great reason to

drive south from Chicago. Located near Danville, about 170 miles from the Loop, the park is an unlikely oasis of hills, trees, lakes and killer off-road bicycle trails maintained by the state's Department of Natural Resources and the Kickapoo Mountain Bike Club.

Kickapoo State Park is said to be the first state park in Illinois to build trails specifically for mountain biking. The first were laid in the early 1990s and now total about 12 miles, almost entirely singletrack.

It doesn't take a visitor long to recognize the area's appeal for mountain biking or why the National Off-Road Bicycling Association has sanctioned races here for several years. At the main entrance, steep bluffs and ravines provide an imposing welcome. Some of the more unusual land formations are remnants of strip mining, which occurred in the area from the 1850s to the 1940s.

The initial part of the trail is twisty, providing in turns what it lacks in elevation. The route is marked with signs that help from accidentally steering onto one of the many bridle or hiking paths it intersects.

Trail sections are numbered, with the first three sections providing a good warm-up for the last three, which have an ample amount of climbs and descents. Section four is especially harrowing, with a precarious bridge crossing followed by a long switchbacked descent that plunges into a deep ravine, bottoms-out through a rocky stream, then snakes back up to the top of the ravine.

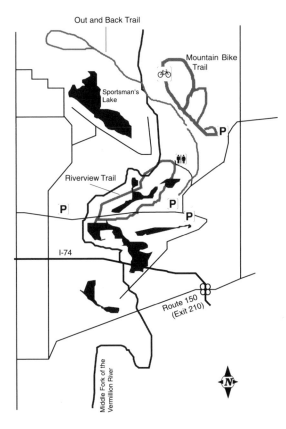

Another highlight of the second half of the trail is where it snakes along the top of a 100-foot bluff. The trail descends through trees and makes furious left and right turns before hitting a succession of woop-de-doos prior to a final last drop.

Several other descents are long enough where speeds can top 30 mph or more. And the climbs are tall enough where you actually have to bear down and climb, rather than let momentum get you halfway up.

While most of the route is wooded,

there are a few short sections where the trail runs adjacent to farmland and prairie. A couple of sections are routed onto gravel roads, but those parts do not last long, either.

In conjunction with approval by the DNR, Kickapoo Mountain Bike Club plans to build about three or four more miles of trails, plus install water bars to help curb erosion on some of the steeper hills.

Many of the routes are adapted from old walking paths and game trails, though a few of the steepest descents were previously motorcycle trails, according to a club spokesman.

Salt Creek
Forest Preserve
(708) 366-9420

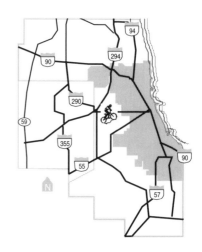

Physical Challenge: ☆
Technical Challenge: ☆☆☆
Singletrack: 40 %
Doubletrack: 20 %
Length: 9+ miles
Distance from Loop: 15 miles
Tread: dirt, gravel, asphalt

Like all quality Chicago area off-road bicycling locations, the trail system along Salt Creek has a single characteristic that sets it apart from all the others.

It's not hills. It's not speed. It's not an incredible burrito joint near the trailhead. More than any other trail within 20 miles of downtown, Salt Creek has turns.

The trail system snakes along the creek through about 3,000 acres managed by the Forest Preserve District of Cook County. Stretching from First Avenue in Brookfield to I-294 near Oak Brook, the system is good for about 10 miles of wooded riding on both sides of the creek, often within feet of its banks.

Further away from the water is a paved bicycle path called the Salt Creek Trail, which starts near the Brookfield Zoo. It's popular with road bikers, in-line skaters and joggers. Mountain bik-

ers use it to ride to the best single-track sections.

Dirt trails along Salt Creek are easily accessed from many locations along the length of the paved trail, with the longest sections starting near its eastern end. Pick them up on the creek's south side and alternate sides as necessary using streets that cut through the preserve.

While the area is about as flat as it gets around Cook County, some area mountain bikers make it their

top spot for a quickie ride.

Many mountain bikers who head from east to west on the south side of the creek turn back at Mannheim Road and head east again, riding on the creek's north side. West of Mannheim, thin trails are less abundant but available for riders willing to look for it, especially in Bemis Woods near the DuPage County line.

The sole elevation change greater than 10 feet is a man-made hill in a patch of trees

called Westchester Woods. It's very steep and high enough to see downtown.

As for the creek itself, it's about six feet deep and 30 feet wide. More winding and scenic than other nearby waterways, such as the DesPlaines River, it took its name a century ago when, legend has it, someone dumped a wagon load of salt into it.

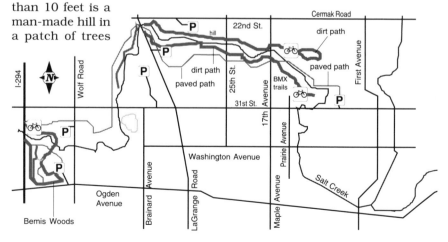

Indian Boundary
Division
(708) 824-1900

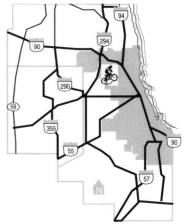

Physical Challenge: ✶✩
Technical Challenge: ✩✩✩
Singletrack: 40 %
Doubletrack: 50 %
Length: 11+ miles
Distance from Loop: 11 miles
Tread: dirt

D on't have a car? The best place to mountain bike within riding distance from the Loop is the Indian Boundary Trail.

The trail runs along the east side of the DesPlaines River between River Forest and O'Hare International Airport and is entirely composed of natural tread surfaces. Save for a few city streets the trail has to cross, there isn't a speck of asphalt. (The Forest Preserve District of Cook County is reportedly looking into paving at least part of the trail as a way to facilitate access.)

A good place to start is near the Grand Avenue bridge in River Grove. The trail actually starts a couple of miles to the south, but if you're coming from the Loop on a bike, Grand is a straight shot.

Get on the trail on the east side of the bridge. The main route is a dirt multipurpose path that runs through trees and shrubs. Heading north, it's moderately challenging all the way to Lawrence Avenue, where

most of the singletrack starts. To find the best sections, stay as close to the river as possible, especially wherever the path forks.

Most of the stretches that appear to branch east, away from the river, lead to parking lots, except between Belmont Avenue and Irving Park Road, where several thin dirt trails lead to a manmade hill about a quarter-mile away from the river. The trails twist through trees making short climbs and descents before heading up the hill. Several other trails lead back to the river.

Between Irving and Lawrence, the trail crosses a stream and a bridge for one of the more technical one-two punches along the entire route heading either north or south.

Near Higgins Road, the singletrack route passes below I-90. About 100 yards to the north, it runs into a cemetery along the river. Get around the fenced-off area by heading east for a quarter mile. The singletrack resumes along the river on the

cemetery's opposite side. This is the only major obstruction along the length of the path.

The multipurpose path crosses I-90 on a bridge about a quarter mile east of the river.

The trail was originally created by Native Americans who used the river for transportation and fishing, and there are a couple of graves along the route.

The grave of one of the area's last Native American chieftain, Che-che-pin-qua, is on the north side of Lawrence near East River Road. There's a maze of singletrack between the river and the stone which marks his grave. To continue from the grave, return to the multipurpose trail or to the river to find the singletrack.

At Touhy Avenue, the trail leaves the Indian Boundary Division of the forest preserve and enters the DesPlaines Division, where it continues north for another 12 miles to the Lake County border.

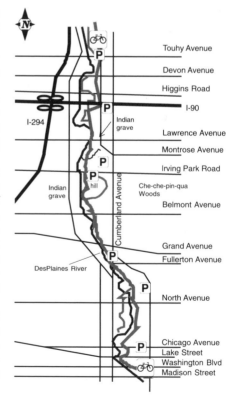

Leroy Oakes
Forest Preserve
(630) 584-5988

Physical Challenge: ☆
Technical Challenge: ☆
Singletrack: 10 %
Doubletrack: 20 %
Length: 5 miles
Distance from Loop: 40 miles
Tread: grass, dirt, wood chips

The U.S. Cycling Federation held its Illinois Cyclo-cross Championships at St. Charles' Leroy Oaks Forest Preserve in 1993 and 1994. Portions of those contests used multipurpose trails that loop the preserve's 256 acres.

Many of the trails are grass and maintained with a lawnmower. This can get confusing where the tread seems to blend into adjacent grasslands, such as along Ferson Creek. There, as well as in other sections, the route seems to disappear.

The area's tree-lined routes are accessible from a couple of parking lots. One is next to the Leroy Oakes barn, and the other is about a hundred yards beyond it to the north. If the second lot is closed, park at the first one and start on the grass trails heading east.

The best part of the trail system is where it enters trees along Randall Road. The route tackles a few hills and makes a handful of gentle turns before spitting out onto the grassy areas along the creek.

Though the trails were not made for mountain bikes, two-wheelers are not prohibited by the Kane County Forest Preserve District.

The 14-mile Great Western Trail starts directly across the street from the preserve. It's made of limestone screenings and is considered the most rural of all Chicago-area rail-trails.

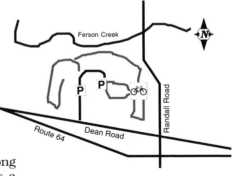

Churchill Woods
Forest Preserve
(630) 790-4900

Physical Challenge: ☆
Technical Challenge: ☆
Singletrack: -
Doubletrack: 35 %
Length: 6 miles
Distance from Loop: 26 miles
Tread: grass

Refer to map at left for trail location.

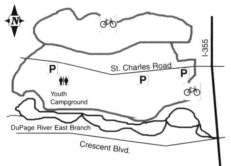

Churchill Woods Forest Preserve near Glen Ellyn has two bike loops that run on either side of St. Charles Road.

The south loop runs partly along the DuPage River and is a flat, scenic cruiser. The route can be difficult to see amid the surrounding grassy fields, but otherwise it's very easy to ride and perfect for riders without much experience off-road.

The north loop is more of a challenge and begins in a heavily wooded area. After about a half mile it moves onto a prairie where it zigzags through tall grass and climbs a very moderate hill. The trail's width is mowed at about eight feet.

The most challenging part of the north loop starts where it leaves the prairie and re-enters the trees. The tread here is dirt and there's a gradual descent for about a mile before the trail ends where it started.

Kankakee River
State Park

(815) 933-1383

Physical Challenge: ✰✰
Technical Challenge: ✰
Singletrack: 35%
Doubletrack: 35%
Length: 7 miles
Distance from Loop: 65 miles
Tread: crushed limestone

Kankakee River State Park has sandstone bluffs, rugged ravines and one of the Chicago area's only suspension bridges for foot traffic and bicycles. Yes, the allure here is scenery.

Located about 65 miles southwest of Chicago, the park envelopes the Kankakee River for about 11 miles. The trail runs parallel to the river through thick woods on its north bank.

Made of crushed limestone, the trail is a breeze to ride, hence its popularity with families. Children, teenagers, adults and seniors are all represented on the trail, as the park attracts about 1.4 million visitors every year. Many come to fish, hunt, hike, and cross-country ski, but a substantial portion bring bikes, some for weekend stays in the park's campgrounds.

In response to the trail's popularity with beginner and intermediate off-roaders, the DNR recently built small rest areas and bike racks along the route. There's a new covered bridge, too, but it doesn't compare to the much larger suspension bridge which spans Rock Creek at a height of about 75 feet and offers the park's most dramatic sights. The creek looks just like the Wisconsin Dells, but without the waterslides and cheese outlets.

The trail can be picked up at numerous parking lots along its length, but the closest lot to Chicago is on its eastern end near Davis Creek Campground. From the trailhead, it heads west, with markers posted every half mile.

It's a smooth cruise through trees until the midway point, where it runs along the river for about a mile.

At Warner Bridge Road, near the park's solitary hill, the crushed limestone gives way to asphalt for another mile before ending in the Chippewa Campground. A 3-mile off-road extension is being added, which will make the total trip from one end of the trail to the other, and

back, a total of 20 miles. Not a huge distance, but more than enough to merit a visit and get a good sweat going.

In addition to the crushed lime-stone route, there are a handful of short stretches of dirt trails along the river. Most are foot trails used by fishermen and they don't last for long.

On the river's south bank, all trails are off-limits to bikes. Detailed maps are available at the park office or in the park's bike rental shop.

Where Rock Creek flows into the river was the site of an extensive Native American village in the late 18th and early 19th centuries, when the Potowatomi, Ottawa and Chippewa nations lived in the area. Nearby is a marker for Chief Shaw-waw-nas-see. In the 17th century, Miami In-dians were so common here that the Kankakee was called the River of the

Miami, according to a park spokes-man.

If the Native American stuff isn't enough history, stop and check out Smith Cemetery, where weathered tombstones mark the graves of early settlers, many of whom died in a yel-low fever epidemic in the early 1800s.

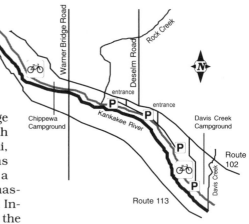

Illinois Beach
State Park
(847) 662-4811

Physical Challenge: ☆
Technical Challenge: ☆
Singletrack: - %
Doubletrack: 10 %
Length: 13 miles
Distance from Loop: 40 miles
Tread: crushed limestone, grass

The sign at the entrance makes it clear: Illinois Beach State Park is located in Illinois. But judging from the cactus and sand dunes visible from the park's bike trail, it could easily be located someplace exotic. Say, Indiana.

Illinois Beach State Park is in Zion, about 40 miles north of Chicago, where the state's only natural beach ridge shoreline stretches for more than six miles along Lake Michigan. Thanks to a scenic 13-mile multi-purpose trail, much of it can be seen by bike.

By steering clear of the sand, the crushed limestone and grass trail system makes for a very leisurely ride. It gives a good look at all 4,200 acres in the park, not including its dedicated nature preserve, which is off-limits.

Since the state's Department of Natural Resources upgraded the trail in the mid-1990s, bicyclists have increased to account for half of all trail users, according to a park spokesman.

Ridges of sand, separated by depressions called "swales," can be seen running parallel to the shore. The swales are home to large expanses of marsh, where cattails, prairie grass and prickly pear cactus coexist with about 650 other plant species, 86 of which are endangered. Illinois Beach has more endangered plant species than any place its size in the entire country, according to the DNR.

One of the most striking sights in the park has nothing to do with vegetation. Try uranium. Twin nuclear reactors operated by Commonwealth Edison until the late 1990s are located at waters' edge and effectively divide the park into northern and southern sections. The station's cooling towers, nearly 200 feet tall, make for great reference points to help avoid getting lost when the lake is out of sight to the east.

From the main parking lot, the trail

leads south through an oak savanna before returning north and coming within eyeshot of the lake. It's a terrific view with a few curves and a couple of modest hills to help build a sweat.

There's about 4 miles of riding available in the Southern Unit, not counting trails located in the nature preserve. Dead River, one of its most peculiar sites, is cut off from the lake by a sand bar and it forms an elongated pond. When the water level rises, the pond breaks through the bar and flows into the lake, draining surrounding marshes.

The tranquillity of the Southern Unit turns troublesome when it's time to move on to the park's Northern Unit. Because there is no direct connection inside the park, the suggested method of traveling between the two points is on the Zion bike path, outside the park. Plans are afoot to someday create a connector trail through ComEd property, but not anytime soon.

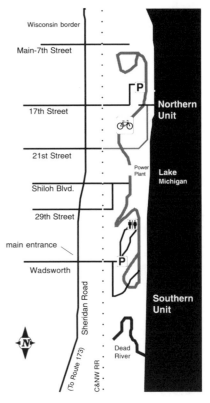

DesPlaines
Division
(708) 824-1900

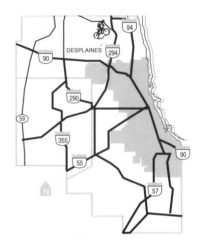

Physical Challenge: ☆ ☆

Technical Challenge: ☆ ☆ ☆

Singletrack: 40 %

Doubletrack: 55 %

Length: 12 miles

Distance from Loop: 15 miles

Tread: dirt, cinders

The DesPlaines Division of the Forest Preserve District of Cook County is one of the best areas for mountain biking in metropolitan Chicago.

This northwest-suburban paradise is nearly unbeatable when it comes to racking up quality miles. It might not be as large as other areas, but because its best trails are so easy to find, you spend less time wondering where to go and more time pedaling.

The DesPlaines Division has about

4,100 acres that envelop the DesPlaines River Valley between Touhy Avenue on the south and Lake-Cook Road on the north. In between, a 12-mile multipurpose trail runs along the east bank of the river with trees and small hills the entire way. In very few spots there are coal cinders embedded into the trail, left over from the 1930s when the Works Progress Administration used them as a cheap way to maintain the path. Otherwise, it's nothing but dirt.

The trail measures between five and 10 feet wide with trees bordering it on both sides. Thinner routes are closer to the river's edge and, depending on the caprice of Mother Nature, can be dry, moist, or completely submerged underwater. When it hasn't rained for awhile, they are lots of fun, with a smooth tread and lots of turns. Though they lack major uphills and downhills, they make gradual elevation

changes that, though small, complete the whole package.

If the thin trails are too wet to ride, the multipurpose trail is nearly always ridable. And because most of the division's trails run north and south, it's nearly impossible to get lost. Unlike other Chicago-area riding locations, where after a few miles on a good trail you get detoured or lost, or get stuck on a loop, you can always keep covering new terrain. Simply head north or south and follow the river.

Another great thing about the DesPlaines Division is its location bordering the north end of the Indian Boundary Division. Both share the same features which can make for an amazing long-distance ride.

The only reason a rider may need to slow are at a half-dozen east-west streets. It's no problem crossing them and picking up the trail on the other side, except at the Northwest Highway. When you run into it, detour west to DesPlaines River Road.

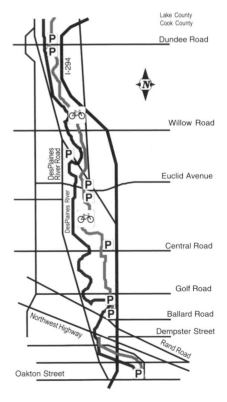

Illinois & Michigan
Canal Trail
(815) 740-2047

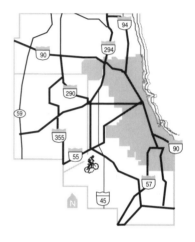

Physical Challenge:	☆
Technical Challenge:	☆ ☆ ☆
Singletrack:	45 %
Doubletrack:	10 %
Length:	9+ miles
Distance from Loop:	23 miles
Tread:	dirt, asphalt

Tucked away on a thin parcel of land directly north of Palos/Sag Valley forest preserves, the Illinois & Michigan Canal Trail is yet another reason to visit the southwest suburbs on a mountain bike.

The I & M Trail is a paved trail that has two 3-mile loops on its eastern and western ends. The Forest Preserve District of Cook County built it in 1971 on a sliver of land that separates the I & M and the Sanitary and Ship canals, which run through a small part of a federally-designated National Heritage Corridor. The trail stretches between LaGrange Road on the east and Route 83 on the west. While it's not very exciting, it provides access to more challenging dirt sections away from the canal.

The most popular spot to start is near Archer Avenue and Willow Springs Road, where there's a parking lot next to the Willow Springs Metra commuter station. The paved route runs through the lot.

Head southwest and look for a dirt detour that branches to the north. There is an obvious one, marked by

cement stumps, about a mile from the lot. Dirt routes fan out from there and squirrel through trees. Nothing fancy or very challenging -- just solid excursions on a developed off-road trail system.

Another option is to access a stretch of singletrack directly north of the parking lot. Here, the trail takes on a few small mounds of earth.

The visitors center near the parking lot explains the history of the National Heritage Corridor. It details how French explorers Louis Jolliet and Jacques Marquette passed through the area in 1673 after traveling the Mississippi River to the Gulf of Mexico. On their return north, they used the Illinois and DesPlaines rivers to head toward Lake Michigan. Near where they carried their canoes from the

DesPlaines to the Chicago River, known today as the Chicago Portage, the I & M was dug in 1843 for cargo vessels to pass from the Great Lakes to the Gulf of Mexico.

Palos/Sag Valley
Forest Preserves
(708) 839-5617

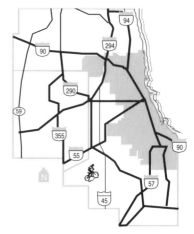

Physical Challenge: ☆☆☆☆
Technical Challenge: ☆☆☆
Singletrack: 45 %
Doubletrack: 45 %
Length: 30+ miles
Distance from Loop: 20 miles
Tread: dirt, gravel, sand

D espite assorted trail closures in 1996, Palos-Sag Valley forest preserves remain the Chicago area's most diverse and challenging riding area.

With 15,000 acres, it dwarfs other riding locations in Cook County in both size and elevation. Several hills here exceed 50 feet, while the longest trails go for miles without interruption.

Although about 20 miles of singletrack were lost to closures, several key trails remain open as a part of the official system, including Three Ravines Trail and Dynamite Road, both of which can be accessed from the Bull Frog Lake parking lot.

The area hardest hit by closures is the entire Sag Valley Division, which forms the southern half of the Palos-Sag Valley area. Every singletrack trail in the division south of Route 83,

where the county's tallest and steepest hills are located, is banned to bikes. Orange markers, which indicate a trail is closed, are positioned at affected trailheads.

While Sag Valley lost most of its technical challenges to trail closures, the division's multipurpose trails are still open, providing the same tough physical challenges that the area built a reputation on. They can still be easily accessed off of

Route 83, 96th Avenue and 104th Avenue.

The Palos Division, which forms the area's northern half, also had singletrack closures but on a more site specific basis. From Bull Frog Lake, a variety of thin, twisty, and hilly trails run through Paw Paw Woods. Bring a patch kit because the trails are long and hard, and they're no place to be stranded.

Many trails that are open to bikes are marked with gray assurance markers, but not all of them.

Eventually, another 26 miles of existing trails, mostly singletrack, are slated to be incorporated into the off-road system as conditions permit. Responsible trail use by riders will go along way when the county decides if, and when, a closed trail should be re-opened.

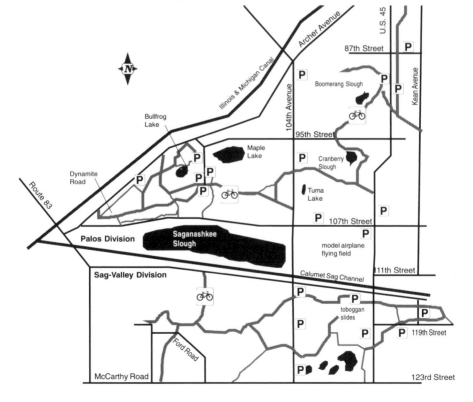

West Branch Reservoir
Trail

(708) 790-4900

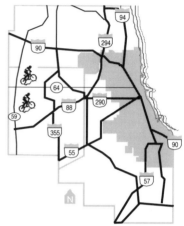

Physical Challenge:	☆
Technical Challenge:	☆ ☆
Singletrack:	40 %
Doubletrack:	15 %
Length:	4 miles
Distance from Loop:	36 miles
Tread:	crushed limestone, grass, dirt

Save for a thin line of trees stretching for about two miles, the West Branch Reservoir Forest Preserve is a wide-open, gently rolling tract in the middle of Chicago's far-western suburbs.

The multipurpose trail winds around two earthen water reservoirs adjacent to the West Branch of the DuPage River. The reservoirs, located in the northern part of the preserve, are separated from the river by less than 10 feet of land for about a mile. The trail runs between them.

Head west from the parking lot on the crushed limestone path and follow it into the trees. The tread narrows after it heads south, getting thinner and thinner until finally it's bordered by water on both sides. Small moguls and tree stumps dot the way.

Because of all the trees and bumps, plus the peculiarity of being surrounded by water, it's a tough path to travel. It requires plenty of maneuvering and tricky pedal work.

The trail forks after a mile or so, one way spitting onto a grassy prairie and circling the other side of a reservoir before heading back to the parking lot. Most of it is grass and runs through open fields.

The other way returns north on another thin land bridge. It's wooded the whole way and in one part requires users to cross a stream.

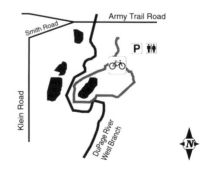

West DuPage
Woods

(708) 790-4900

Physical Challenge: ☆ ☆
Technical Challenge: ☆
Singletrack: - %
Doubletrack: 15 %
Length: 11 miles
Distance from Loop: 35 miles
Tread: gravel, grass

Refer to map at left, top biker, for trail location.

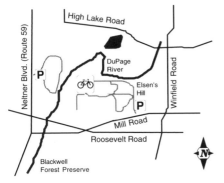

West DuPage Woods in Winfield is as ideal a spot as any for a ride in DuPage County forest preserves. The grass and gravel trails and main topographical feature, Elsen's Hill, make for moderate fun along an innocuous slope along the West Branch of the DuPage River.

There are four color-coded loops that circle West DuPage Woods' 470 acres. It's packed with oak trees but there are a few open fields and marshes that add scenic variety.

The area's greatest elevation changes are on Elsen's Hill, where separate trails climb and descend up to 40 feet. The hill forms a gradual half-mile slope that leads down and away from the parking lot, so it's not visible from a distance. At its base is the river, along which run the area's twistiest trails.

The only problem for bicyclists at Elsen's Hill is that the area is primarily used by local land owners for horseback riding. The horses leave a lot of hoof marks, which can make it rough.

Plans are afoot to connect the woods to a regional county trail system, which includes the Great Western Trail, the Illinois Prairie Path and nearby trails in Blackwell Forest Preserve.

LaBagh Woods

(312) 261-8400

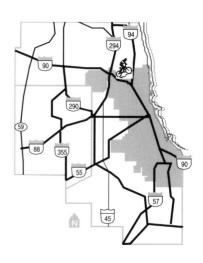

Physical Challenge: ☆
Technical Challenge: ☆ ☆
Singletrack: 35 %
Doubletrack: 20 %
Length: 5+ miles
Distance from Loop: 9 miles
Tread: dirt

LaBagh Woods, at Foster and Cicero avenues in Chicago, has several miles of dirt trails that run along the North Branch of the Chicago River. They're far from secret -- the U.S. Cycling Federation sanctioned cyclo-cross events on them for 10 years until the Forest Preserve District of Cook County nixed the events due to erosion concerns.

These wiry trails, located near the southern end of the paved North Branch Bicycle Trail, have a variety of twists and turns. Not very long, but pretty good for being in the middle of the Northwest Side. They provide one of the few quality outlets for city bikers who don't have a car to drive someplace more remote.

An easy way to enter LaBagh Woods is off Cicero, just north of Foster. Turn into the woods on an overpass above I-94 and stay to the left to get to a picnic shelter. A trailhead near the shelter leads into the woods before splitting and heading north and south along the west bank of the river.

Additional trails are located on the river's opposite side, as well as on both sides of a pair of railroad tracks which cut through the preserve. The action ends at about Miltmore Street on the north.

There are more dirt trails west of Central Avenue, north of Devon Avenue, adjacent to the North Branch Trail in Caldwell Woods. Caldwell Woods is named in honor of Billy Caldwell, a mixed-race Potawatomi chief who played a role in saving the lives of several early Chicago pioneers during the Ft. Dearborn massacre in 1812.

Save for the singletrack that can be found in LaBagh and Caldwell woods, the North Branch Bicycle Trail is paved and flat. Its ideal uses are for in-line skating and road biking. The trail's northern terminus is at the Chicago Botanic Gardens in the Skokie Division of the Forest Preserve District.

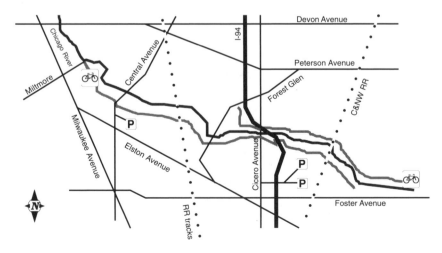

Waterfall Glen
Forest Preserve
(708) 790-4900

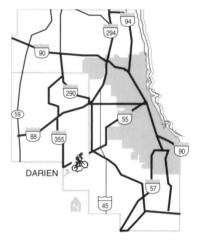

Physical Challenge: ☆ ☆
Technical Challenge: ☆ ☆
Singletrack: -- %
Doubletrack: -- %
Length: 8+ miles
Distance from Loop: 25 miles
Tread: limestone screenings, dirt

W aterfall Glen is appropriately touted by the Forest Preserve District of DuPage County as its best place to mountain bike. There are miles of multi-purpose trails that make a winding, rolling loop around Argonne National Laboratory.

For scenery, there's plenty of limestone bluffs, rocky outcroppings, savannas, pine groves, valleys, an artesian well, waterfall and Signal Hill -- high enough for Native Americans to have used as a vantage point to send long-distance signals.

While a county ordinance prohibits two wheelers on the preserve's thinnest trails, the multipurpose paths are big-time fun, with elevation changes more than 30 feet. And thanks to a hard, crushed limestone surface, it's fast. Riders of all ability levels enjoy this place.

For die-hard singletrack lovers, it can get a bit frustrating. A couple of dirt off-

shoots from the main trail have the eight-foot width required by a county ordinance for bikes, yet they eventually narrow to just a couple of feet. Confronted with a demand by local riders, the county is reportedly considering opening up a stretch or two of singletrack for mountain bikers. Check with the county for updated trail policies.

Besides scenery, the area has a long history. It provided the limestone used for Chicago's historic water tower, trees for the city's Lincoln

Park, and earth to expand its lakefront. Prior to 1800, it was home to trappers and traders, including a guy named DuPahze, for whom the county was named. The name Waterfall Glen, incidentally, isn't derived from the falls in the southwestern

part of the preserve. The preserve is actually named after Seymour "Bud" Waterfall, an early president of the district's board of commissioners.

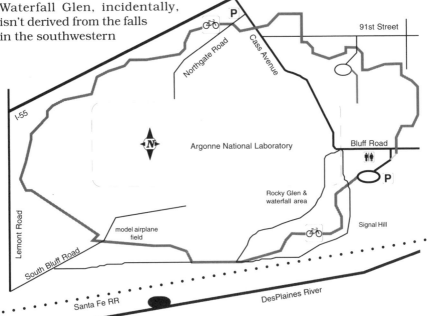

Deer Grove
Forest Preserve
(708) 366-9420

Physical Challenge:	✰ ✰
Technical Challenge:	✰ ✰ ✰
Singletrack:	40 %
Doubletrack:	25 %
Length:	8+ miles
Distance from Loop:	30 miles
Tread:	dirt, gravel, asphalt

Deer Grove Forest Preserve is to the northwest suburbs what Palos/Sag Valley forest preserves are to the southwest suburbs, but not as hilly or big.

Located near Palatine, there are about 1,800 acres in Deer Grove, all part of the Forest Preserve District of Cook County's Northwest Division. The majority of the preserve is on the west side of Quentin Road, but there's plenty to explore on the east side, too. At least two or three visits are required to explore the whole thing.

Like many Chicago area forest preserves, there is an abundance of dirt trails here, but finding them can be difficult if you don't know where you're going.

There is a parking lot on Quentin Road, between Dundee and Lake-Cook roads, that has several miles of dirt trails nearby. It's adjacent to an area called Camp Reinberg. Ride west from the parking lot, across Quentin, on the preserve's 4-mile

bike path -- one of the eight designated bike paths in the county system. It's made of asphalt, but after about 75 yards, there is a dirt trail that branches off to the right. A yellow Cook County Forest Preserve sign marks the trailhead. From this long, undulating cruiser, a number of other dirt trails are accessible.

Expect to find rolling, upland forests interspersed with wetlands, ravines and shallow creeks which feed the preserve's two lakes.

Deer Grove is great for long stretches of uninterrupted trails, many of which run through shallow ravines and make brief stream crossings. Advanced riders might find them amusing, but novices will have their hands full.

An area called Deer Grove East, east of Quentin, has a paved bike trail, as well as an off-road path.

As the one of the county's oldest forest preserve holdings, special trail policies were recently adopted here. Watch for signs that indicate if a trail is closed to bikes.

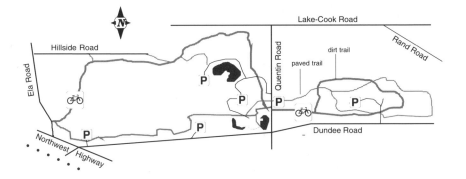

Chicago
Lakefront Bike Path
(312) 294-2200

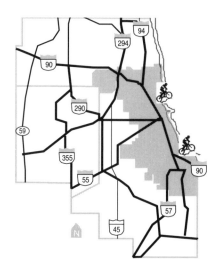

Physical Challenge: ☆
Technical Challenge: ☆
Singletrack: 25 %
Doubletrack: 5 %
Length: 20 miles
Distance from Loop: .5 miles
Tread: asphalt, dirt, grass,
                cinders

The Lakefront Bike Path is a 20-mile-long swath of asphalt between Hollywood Avenue on the north and 71st Street on the south. Probably the best things about it are the views it affords of the Chicago skyline and lakefront beaches. Because just about everyone loves it for these primary reasons, traffic is heavy during summer weekends. Don't be shocked if you have to dismount and walk, especially near North Avenue and Oak Street beaches, where road bikers, in-line skaters, walkers and joggers compete for space.

Off-roaders can avoid other users by sticking to long stretches of developed singletrack that run adjacent to the main path for much of its distance. There's also a cinder bridle path that, in spots, runs parallel to the asphalt.

On the North Side, singletrack is particularly well developed between North Avenue Beach and Diversey Harbor, and between Belmont Har-

bor and Montrose Harbor. The route is fairly flat, except for Cricket Hill and Prospect Hill in Lincoln Park.

On the South Side, singletrack stretches most of the way from 31st Street to Promontory Point at 55th Street. From there, the dirt route is spotty to the South Shore Yacht Club at 71st Street.

There are more man-made hills on the South Side than on the North Side, especially south of 31st Street. Of course, the elevations aren't huge -- just 20 feet or so -- but they can be challenging on a long ride or facing a stiff headwind.

In 1998, the Chicago Department of Transportation plans on adding new crosswalks where the path intersects with streets. Similar to speed bumps, the new crosswalks are being designed to eliminate the potential for collisions between trail users and motorized vehicles that enter the park without stopping at stop signs.

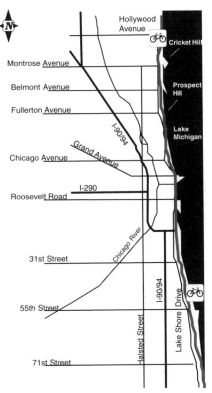

Chipilly Woods

(847) 446-5652

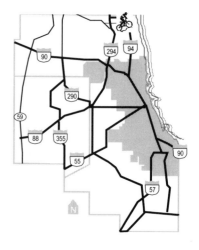

Physical Challenge:	☆
Technical Challenge:	☆
Singletrack:	50 %
Doubletrack:	10 %
Length:	6 miles
Distance from Loop:	27 miles
Tread:	dirt, gravel

Chipilly Woods is the larger of two small trail systems on Dundee Road in Northbrook. But unlike its little brother, Somme Woods, Chippily can be a bit confusing. Its trail system runs in several directions and is crisscrossed by the Middle Fork of the North Branch of the Chicago River and a set of railroad tracks. A compass comes in real handy here.

From the trailhead on Dundee, the route winds south on tight singletrack to the Middle Fork, passes beneath the railroad tracks and snakes along the river's north bank for a couple of miles. It's easy to return along another path about 30 yards from the water.

Trails on the south side of the river run through the heart of Chipilly Woods. The trail is almost entirely singletrack with a few tiny hills and a couple of stream-crossings. It eventually dumps into a wide-open, grassy field with a marker commemorating WWI battles on Chipilly Ridge in France.

Trails on the east side of the tracks, also south of the river, have the largest elevation changes, with hills and clims up to 10 feet.

To get to Somme Woods, head west for a mile on Dundee.

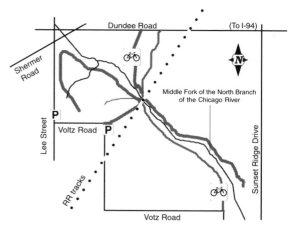

Somme Woods

(847) 446-5652

Physical Challenge: ☆
Technical Challenge: ☆
Singletrack: 50 %
Doubletrack: 30 %
Length: 3+ miles
Distance from Loop: 28 miles
Tread: dirt

Refer to map at left for trail location.

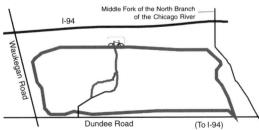

Just 30 miles north of downtown, where the Middle Fork of the North Branch of the Chicago River flows through Somme Woods, is a brief, off-road trail system that North Shore riders have been enjoying for a while now.

Named in honor of U.S. victories during WWI along the Somme River in France, the woods has a dirt multi-purpose path that makes a rectangular loop around its perimeter. The path is flat and easy, although ruts and blowdowns jazz things up in spots. A moderately technical stretch of singletrack serves as the lone detour, cutting through huge stands of oak, elm and maple trees in the middle of the loop.

The south side of the loop runs parallel to Dundee Road, and part of the west side leaves the woods and runs near the curb on Waukegan Road. The north side of the preserve is bordered by an east-west stretch of I-94.

An easy place to get started when arriving by car is at the Somme Woods parking lot on Dundee.

The Middle Fork, as its name implies, is the middle of three arms of the North Branch of the Chicago River. There's also a West Fork and an East Fork, sometimes referred to as the Skokie River. All three forks head south and join near Glenview.

Moraine Hills
State Park

(815) 385-1624

Physical Challenge:

Technical Challenge:

Singletrack: -- %

Doubletrack: -- %

Length: 8 miles

Distance from Loop: 60 miles

Tread: limestone screenings

L ocated in McHenry County, Mo- raine Hills State Park lies on the same 100-mile-long moraine as the famous Kettle Moraine State Forest in southern Wisconsin. The major difference between these areas is that Moraine Hills' trails are made of crushed limestone rather than dirt.

There are three different moun- tain bike loops to choose from in the park, which opened in 1976. The longest is the Lake Defiance Trail. Nearly 4 miles long, it circles 48-acre Lake Defiance, one of the largest un- developed glacial lakes in the state. About halfway around the lake it connects with the 2-mile Fox River Trail, which partly runs along the Fox River and provides access to the McHenry Dam in the southwest cor- ner of the park.

The 3-mile Leather Leaf Bog Trail has the most turns of the three des- ignated bike paths. It winds around typical moraine topography, includ- ing kettles, which are surface de-

pressions, and kames, which are conical hills shaped by glacial melt- water. These features account for the nearly 1 million visitors that visit the park each year. Many of them arrive as families for a group ride.

Each trail is about 10 feet wide and, save for an occasional wash- out or blowdown across the trail, the tread is smooth and easy to ride. Riders that are just discovering off- road bicycling, however, may find them difficult.

Physically, the park's rolling hills can turn into leg-burners when tackled in succession. The highest point in the park is 790 feet above sea level, or about 40 feet higher than surrounding plains.

Bikers who like to stop frequently to appreciate their surroundings won't be disappointed here because the park has two federally desig- nated nature preserves. But don't get carried away with exploration. Park rangers are adamant that rid- ers remain on the designated loops.

Trailblazers are subject to a $75 fine.

A good spot to start is at the Northern Lakes Day Use parking area at the end of the main road which leads past the park's main entrance. All three trails are accessible from there and each runs one-way.

Roughly half of the park's 1,690 acres are wetlands and lakes. One area, Pike Marsh in the southeast corner, supports one of the state's largest pitcher plant colonies. Take a breather and watch these plants attract, trap and digest insects.

More than 100 bird species have been identified in the park, including several varieties of waterfowl such as mallard and Canada geese. As for mammals, there's red fox, opossum, raccoon, mink and whitetail deer.

Admission is free.

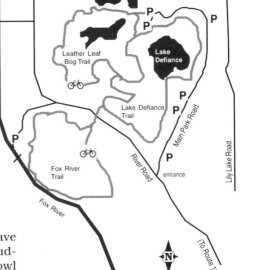

Arie Crown
Forest Preserve
(708) 366-9420

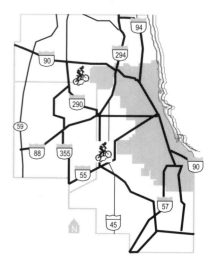

Physical Challenge: ☆
Technical Challenge: ☆ ☆
Singletrack: 35 %
Doubletrack: 65 %
Length: 3+ miles
Distance from Loop: 17 miles
Tread: dirt, grass, gravel

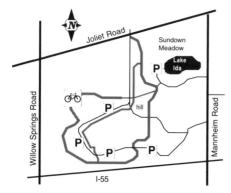

Of the eight official bike trails in the Cook County forest preserve system, Arie Crown preserve's is the only one that isn't paved. Made of dirt, it's about eight feet wide and more than 3 miles long.

The trail forms a couple of internal loops which meander about the preserve's 250 acres. None of them are very hilly but they're more challenging than the paved routes found elsewhere in the county system.

Start near Sundown Meadow off Mannheim Road, just north of 67th Street. From there, multi-purpose trails fan out to the north, south and west. A moderate amount of bumps, rocks and fallen branches keep it interesting for beginner and intermediate riders. There's also a handful of singletrack trails that run through tall grass near Lake Ida.

Busse Woods
Forest Preserve

(800) 870-3666

Physical Challenge: ☆ ☆ ☆
Technical Challenge: ☆ ☆
Singletrack: 35%
Doubletrack: 20%
Length: 12+ miles
Distance from Loop: 25 miles
Tread: dirt, gravel, asphalt

Refer to map at left, top biker, for trail location.

Busse Woods, part of Ned Brown Forest Preserve near O'Hare International Airport, has what is perhaps the largest man-made hill in the Cook County forest preserve system. About 100 feet tall and massive, it's one of the few area hills that make riders grind, and keep grinding, to make it to the top. Forget about using momentum to get you halfway there. It's pure pedal power and balance.

The hill, all 1 million cubic yards of it, was built from soil excavated in the construction of Busse Lake in the early 1970s. Though there's been a certain amount of settling of dirt over time, it's still a monster to climb.

Four dirt trails lead to the top through tall grass. Novices can get near the top on the easiest ones, but the steepest route is for experts exclusively.

Trails to the top come from separate portions of the park's southwest corner. They can be accessed from parking lots off of Bisner Road, about one mile north of Biesterfield Road.

There are dirt trails in other parts of the preserve that lead from various spots along the length of its 12-mile paved path, especially north of Higgins Road. Keep an eye out for the county's only herd of elk near Higgins and Arlington Heights Road.

Dirt trails in a nature preserve in the northernmost portion of the preserve (not shown on map) are off-limits to bikes.

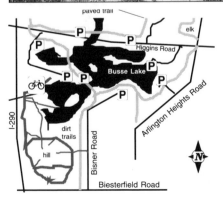

Beverly Lake

(847) 366-9420

Physical Challenge: ☆ ☆
Technical Challenge: ☆
Singletrack: 35 %
Doubletrack: 35 %
Length: 3 miles
Distance from Loop: 35 miles
Tread: dirt, grass

Mountain bikers love superlatives when it comes to describing off-road bicycling locations. "Highest," "longest" and "fastest" are a few of the sexier adjectives for trails around Chicago.

Spring Creek Valley Forest Preserve, home of Penny Road Pond and Beverly Lake, claims a couple of titles. It ranks as the "farthest Cook County forest preserve from the Loop" and, due to miles of uncharted trails, the county's "most obscure" off-road bicycling location.

Characterized by a patchwork of rolling hills, prairie and savanna sewn together by long threads of singletrack, Spring Creek Valley looks easy to get wrapped up in. The key is finding a place to park.

The only trails mapped by the county are at Beverly Lake ski trails, located at the very southern end of the preserve on Higgins Road.

Comprised of a few small loops, the trail is wide and grassy and tackles a few moderate hills.

Small signs indicate the difficulty level of each loop. Most signs precede "easy" and "more difficult" climbs. The largest hills are not huge, just 30 feet or so, but high enough to use a granny gear on the upsides and brakes on the downsides.

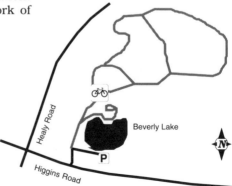

Penny Road Pond

(847) 366-9420

The bulk of Spring Creek Valley Forest Preserve's trails are at Penny Road Pond.

With an estimated 20 miles of trails, a complete exploration lasts from several hours to several days.

From the Penny Road Pond parking lot, trails can be picked up leading northwest, east and south.

The east trails start across the street from the lot. The route has a stream crossing, followed by miles of partly wooded, partly wide-open riding. The tread is mostly single-track but often splits to double-track and triple-track. Numerous detours offer opportunities to get wonderfully lost.

With a lot of horse traffic, the tread is bumpy, however plenty of sections smooth out.

The north route, which also starts across the street from the lot, makes a brief climb and a quick descent before zigzagging into the preserve. It eventually crosses an abandoned road and enters a series of small, technical loops and continues north along the preserve's western border. Heading north of Donlea Road, watch out for a dedicated nature preserve, which is off-limits to bikes.

Trails leading south can be reached by first heading east on

Physical Challenge:	☆☆
Technical Challenge:	☆☆
Singletrack:	80 %
Doubletrack:	10 %
Length:	20+miles
Distance from Loop:	35 miles
Tread:	dirt, grass

Refer to map at left for trail location.

Penny Road. They start on the south side of the road, hook up with a gravel path, then lead to dirt trails good for several miles.

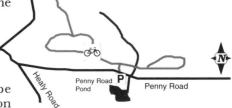

McHenry County
Prairie Trail North

(815) 678-4431

Physical Challenge: ☆
Technical Challenge: ☆
Singletrack: - %
Doubletrack: 5 %
Length: 7.5 miles
Distance from Loop: 70 miles
Tread: dirt, original ballast

There are numerous trails created from abandoned railroad corridors in northern Illinois. One of the only ones with a dirt tread is the McHenry County Prairie Trail North, which runs through rolling farmland.

The trail starts about 75 miles from Chicago in Ringwood on the north side of Barnard Mill Road. Not to be confused with the McHenry County Prairie Trail South, which is paved and located in the southern part of the county, the northern section runs north and south through open fields before it terminates just beyond the Wisconsin border.

Regardless of weather conditions, the dirt and ballast surface is usually dry due to excellent water runoff it receives from being atop a railroad bed with drainage ditches on either side. Some of the most inter-

esting parts of the trail are where it crosses streams on original railroad bridges. And because there is so much bird and animal life nearby, a biker never knows what he or she will see next.

The trail was established in 1987 when the McHenry County Conservation District removed tracks laid by the Chicago & Northwestern railroad to create a trail between the town of Ringwood and the Wisconsin state line. The trail is like a linear park, permitting horseback

riding, hiking, snowmobiling, cross country skiing and mountain biking. An estimated 22,000 people use the trail every year.

An area called Glacial Park, located about a half mile from the trail off of Hart's Road, is a frequent detour for trail users. Though bicyclists are not allowed to venture from the paved areas in the park, it has vistas of some of northern Illinois' most scenic wetlands.

The path is one of 29 rail-trails in the state that total 342 to miles. More than 200 more miles are in the planning stages. Because the state's rail-trails are made with different agreements between municipalities and the railroads that own the corridors, a few differences exist. Some have a lot of signage, while others, like the McHenry Country Prairie Trail North, are more rustic.

The corridor for the trail is leased for $1 a year from Metra, the commuter rail service of the Regional Transportation Authority.

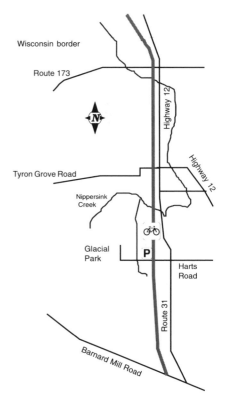

Wisconsin border

Route 173

Highway 12

Highway 12

Tyron Grove Road

Nippersink Creek

Glacial Park

P

Harts Road

Route 31

Barnard Mill Road

MacDonald
Forest Preserve
(847) 367-6640

Physical Challenge: ☆ ☆
Technical Challenge: ☆
Singletrack: - %
Doubletrack: - %
Length: 50 miles
Distance from Loop: 3+ miles
Tread: crushed granite,
                    wood chips

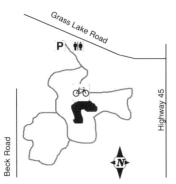

MacDonald Forest Preserve near suburban Lindenhurst has a short, hilly trail that has two seperate loops.

The main loop is an eight-foot-wide crushed granite path. It circles a pond and runs along the fringe of thick stands of trees. There's a bridge across a stream and a handful of relatively steep climbs and descents exceeding 20 feet. Besides being moderately challenging, the hills offer nice views of adjacent prairies and trees.

The second loop is made of wood chips. It's thinner than the main loop and the hills are a bit bigger and more difficult, partly due to the added resistance of the wood chips. Scenery is the same lush, gently rolling landscape. Parts of the trail runs near dense woods adjacent to residential areas.

Grant Woods
Forest Preserve
(847) 367-6640

Physical Challenge: ☆ ☆
Technical Challenge: ☆
Singletrack: - %
Doubletrack: - %
Length: 6 miles
Distance from Loop: 55 miles
Tread: crushed granite

Refer to map at left, bottom biker, for location.

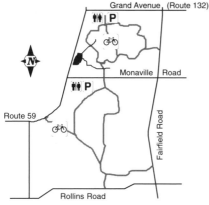

Grant Woods straddles Monaville Road in suburban Lindenhurst. Its north and south sections closely resemble each other, but the south section is older, dating back to the mid-1980s, when it was acquired by the Lake County Forest Preserve District from local farmers and land owners. The north section opened in 1996. Today the preserve totals 974 acres.

Both sections have an eight-foot-wide multipurpose trail that meanders across rolling prairie and through tall stands of trees.

Its primary appeal is scenery, something trail planners kept in mind during construction. According to a forest preserve spokesman, crushed granite was used for the surface for aesthetic reasons. Besides being durable, crushed granite has a creamy color that is easier on the eyes than crushed limestone, which has a white appearance that can be close to blinding on a bright day.

The north section of the trail is 2.5 miles. It's an easy ride save for a few of the bigger hills, which exceed 20 feet. Though there are no technical challenges, there's a couple of bridges which add variety to the ride.

The south section, at 3.5 miles, is a nice cruiser with more hills and long-distance views. In addition to its main loop, there's a couple of branches which dead-end at adjacent streets.

Terrific for a rainy-day ride, the trail is built with a crown that provides excellent water runoff. Even on wet days there's few puddles.

Knoch Knolls Park

(630) 357-9000

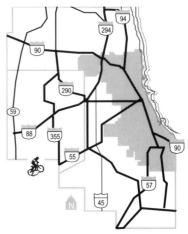

Physical Challenge: ☆
Technical Challenge: ☆
Singletrack: 30 %
Doubletrack: 45 %
Length: 6 miles
Distance from Loop: 45 miles
Tread: dirt, gravel

Squeezed between the east and west branches of the DuPage River near 95th Street and Plainfield Road in Naperville, Knock Knolls Park's 183 acres are a surprising contrast to the farmland and residential subdivisions that surround them. While the horizon is so flat it's almost eerie, the park is a nice little getaway that's almost completely surrounded by water.

As an occasional host to cyclo-cross races, the park has miles of wooded trails, much of it on a cross-country ski system with grass and dirt surfaces. A portion runs along the two rivers, which are parallel to each other and separated by a half mile.

At six to seven feet wide, the multi-purpose paths here are thinner than most ski trails, and in many spots the trails narrow into tight, twisty little corridors. There's also a couple of gravel service roads which run throughout the park. Maintained by the Naperville Park District, all the trails here, regardless of width, are open to bikes.

Elevations changes in the system are moderate, with the largest about 10 feet.

At one point, a gravel trail makes a gradual descent directly into the West Branch, then emerges on the other bank about 30 yards away. It looks like you could pedal straight through, but think again. It's for horses.

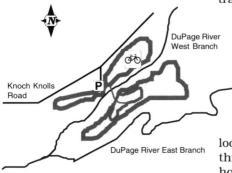

SOUTHERN WISCONSIN

PART II

Greenbush
Recreation Area
(414) 626-2116

Physical Challenge:	☆☆☆☆
Technical Challenge:	☆☆☆
Singletrack:	60 %
Doubletrack:	25 %
Total Distance:	11 miles
Distance from Loop:	150 miles
Tread:	dirt, sand

Greenbush Recreation Area is one of two developed trail systems in the northern unit of the Kettle Moraine State Forest. It boasts four mountain bike trails: the .7-mile Pink Loop, 1.5-mile Red Loop, 3.6-mile Green Loop and 5.1-mile Yellow Loop.

All the trails are well marked, about 10 feet wide and traverse very hilly ground. Some sections run through sunken, kettle-like depressions and climb and descend more than 75 feet. The tread is dirt with a

lot of imbedded rocks.

The hardest loops are Yellow and Pink, with Green and Red good for beginner and intermediate riders. Though the trail corridor is wide enough for cross-country skiers, the turns are tight and challenging, especially at high speeds coming down steep descents.

The system is as challenging as either of the two trail clusters in the southern unit of the state forest, but without as many erosion controls. Here, erosion control devices are limited to water bars and limestone screenings. No rubber mats.

To limit erosion, maintenance crews, including volunteers from the Greenbush Trail Advisory Committee, are experimenting with soil used to fill ruts. To give the soil "staying power" on steep slopes, clay and gravel is added. So far it seems to be working.

Another anti-erosion technique is maintaining the trail to just one side of the corridor. Keeping riders to the left or right limits repair work, as does keeping the trail closed to bikes for much of the year. Trails often aren't open until late April.

So few people visit Greenbush with bikes that the Wisconsin Department of Natural Resources doesn't bother to keep track of ridership statistics. Greenbush's two parking lots are never more than a quarter full except during snow months, when cross-country skiers flock to the area. On an annual basis, skiers are estimated to outnumber bikers by at least 10-to-1, a DNR spokesman said. Trail passes are required.

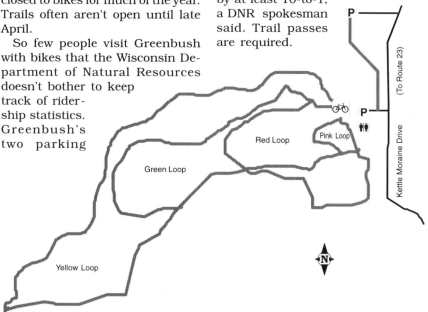

New Fane
Trails

(414) 626-2116

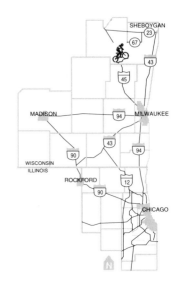

Physical Challenge:	☆ ☆ ☆
Technical Challenge:	☆ ☆ ☆
Singletrack:	55 %
Doubletrack:	20 %
Total Distance:	7+ miles
Distance from Loop:	130 miles
Tread:	dirt, sand

The New Fane trail system lies on part of the 100-mile-long moraine that cuts through the Kettle Moraine State Forest. The Wisconsin Department of Natural Resources claims the moraine, deposited by a glacier more than 10,000 years ago, is one of North America's largest and longest.

Though the trails in the cluster are probably the least visited in the whole forest, it doesn't mean they aren't fun. Unlike the long climbs and fast descents at Greenbush, Emma Carlin, John Muir, or even Lapham Peak, the hills here are short but sweet.

There are four routes to choose from: the .7-mile Brown Loop, 1.5-mile Green Loop, 3.1-mile Yellow Loop and 2.4-mile Red Loop. They're wide, made of dirt and grass and partially strewn with rocks. Most sections are smooth but several stretches are bone jarring. Suspended bikes are made for this sort of terrain.

All the routes are marked with signs to keep trail users abreast of their progress through the dense woods.

Near the parking lot, the trails are sur-

rounded by small hills. Farther away from the lot, the landscape flattens out a bit and the trail plods through pine trees and tall grass. Singletrack runs down the center of the corridor but becomes less defined.

The hardest loop is Yellow. It has a handful of small hills and leads through a pine plantation on its west side. It eventually flattens out and ends up running through upland brush.

While the trails are almost always empty on summer weekdays, even weekend crowds are sparse, at least until snow season. The system is a big draw for cross-country skiers.

If visiting from Chicago on a day trip, it's a good bet to visit nearby Greenbush cluster first, then hit New Fane on the way back home. And be sure to bring a road map. Roads in the area have a lot of turns that make it easy to get lost.

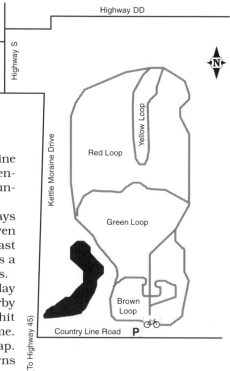

John Muir
Trails

(414) 594-6200

Physical Challenge: ☆☆☆☆

Technical Challenge: ☆☆☆☆

Singletrack: 60 %

Doubletrack: 20 %

Total Distance: 28 miles

Distance from Loop: 90 miles

Tread: dirt, sand

There is something beguiling about the first turn at John Muir Ski and Bike Trails. The turn itself is unspectacular -- just a soft left -- but because it leads into the thick of the Kettle Moraine State Forest, it's hard not to shift into high gear. If you don't shift, expect to be passed by many other trail users.

Perhaps more than any other off-road bicycling location around Chicago, the John Muir trail system requires smart riding. Come here relying on strength, stamina or balance alone and it will be a very long day.

Muir has five loops that were laid out as hiking trails in the 1960s by the Wisconsin Department of Natural Resources with help from the Sierra Club. To settle user conflicts that coincided with the rapid growth of mountain biking in the area, the DNR adopted trail regulations in the early 1990s. To compensate for lost mileage, the DNR, along with volunteer groups, added five miles to Muir

in 1994 and built a new connector trail to nearby Emma Carlin trails.

There's plenty of physical challenges, including steep uphill climbs that can cause fits for the uninitiated. The most grueling have a 23 percent grade that lasts for about 100 feet, a DNR spokesman said. How steep is 23 percent? So steep that only the most elite bikers can make it to the top without stopping.

The 2-mile Red Loop, with only one short downhill, is good for beginners. The 4.8-mile Orange Loop is a bit more challenging with several steep hills, but it's still not as difficult as the 7.4-mile Green Loop. That one is loaded with rocky downhill and uphill runs that require talent, stamina and just a bit of guts. Plan on a lot of gear changing and breaking to compensate for the constantly changing terrain.

Two other routes were recently completed at John Muir: the 4-mile White Loop and the 10-mile Blue Loop. Each has the same barrage of

adversities that make the other loops such a blast.

According to a recent study, about 60,000 riders pass through Muir every year. The numbers reflect that Kettle Moraine State Forest is one of the busiest mountain bike locations in the country, other than Moab in Utah.

Muir often attracts more riders than its sister system Emma Carlin because it is larger, more conveniently accessed from Chicago, has a larger parking area and, unlike Carlin's many rugged sections, is slightly easier for beginners.

Call ahead for trail conditions, especially in the spring.

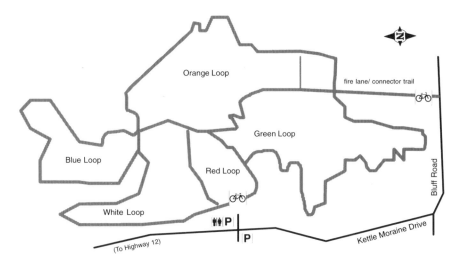

Milwaukee
Lakefront
(414) 257-6100

Physical Challenge:	★ ☆ ☆
Technical Challenge:	☆ ☆
Singletrack:	75 %
Doubletrack:	25 %
Total Distance:	5 miles
Distance from Loop:	94 miles
Tread:	dirt, gravel

The Milwaukee lakefront is a lot like Chicago's lakefront with beaches and parks. The main difference is that Milwaukee's beaches are located at the base of a steep, 75-foot bluff. To the delight of Brew Town bikers, there are a handful of dirt trails that lead straight up and down the slope.

An easy area to sniff them out is near Bradford Beach, a couple of miles north of downtown. Park at the beach lot and use an asphalt trail to get to the top of the bluff. You can attempt to climb the dirt trails, but they are extremely steep. They're a lot easier going down than up, but even going down takes a lot of skill and agility.

In addition to the trails that go straight up and down, other dirt routes reach the top through ravines in the side of the bluff. Some lead to Lakeside Park, where even more trails run through shallow valleys and over small, steep hills.

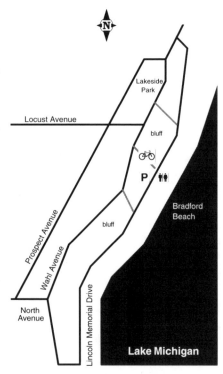

Milwaukee
River
(414) 257-6100

Physical Challenge: ☆ ☆

Technical Challenge: ☆ ☆ ☆

Singletrack: 65 %

Doubletrack: 20 %

Total Distance: 14 miles

Distance from Loop: 94 miles

Tread: dirt, gravel, debris

Refer to map at left for trail location.

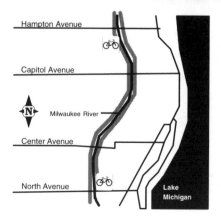

Milwaukee's best mountain biking area is along the Milwaukee River. The river runs north and south and flows through downtown, much like the North Branch of the Chicago River flows into downtown Chicago. The banks of the Milwaukee River are lined with singletrack for 14 miles, or about 7 miles on each side.

The singletrack's southern end is near North Avenue on the East Side. The northern end is north of Capitol Drive. Asphalt and gravel railtrails continue further south and connect with the lakefront about two miles away.

The singletrack is brutal. In spots it runs just a few feet from water's edge but in others it climbs and descends little hills. The usual assortment of natural obstacles are all there, big rocks especially, plus weird stuff like steel rebars and cement bricks sticking out of the dirt. They're usually not noticeable until after they've popped a tire. There are not many bike stores near the river for repairs, so be sure to bring a patch kit and a spare tube or two.

The Milwaukee River does have a couple of strikes against it. The muddy parts have an odor which, after fouling your riding clothes, will send people running. And if waterborn insects aren't your bag, consider visiting in the spring or fall. During summer, be sure to bring bug spray.

Hampton Avenue

Capitol Avenue

N

Milwaukee River

Center Avenue

North Avenue

Lake
Michigan

Governor Dodge
State Park

(608) 935-2315

Physical Challenge: ☆☆☆
Technical Challenge: ☆☆
Singletrack: 30 %
Doubletrack: 20 %
Total Distance: 10+ miles
Distance from Loop: 190 miles
Tread: grass, dirt, asphalt

Governor Dodge State Park is in a unique area of south-central Wisconsin that looks nothing at all like surrounding farmland. Rocky bluffs, steep hills and lots of trees spread out for more than 5,000 acres.

The park's two designated mountain bike trails are open May 1 to Nov. 15, unless posted otherwise. Each one forms a loop that starts and ends in the Cox Hollow Lake parking lot.

The Mill Creek Trail is hilly and short. It starts on asphalt, then leads onto a 12-foot-wide grass path. A thin, dirt tread is starting to develop down the path's center in a few spots, but otherwise, the rest of the 3.3-mile route is as plush as a suburban lawn. Most of it skirts outside the park's wooded areas and instead runs in the open.

The 6.8-mile Meadow Valley Trail is a different story. Singletrack stretches for most of the distance, leading up and down some challenging grades and through tricky turns.

A small part of it runs atop sandstone bluffs and the last two miles are wildly undulating. Nothing terribly technical because it has to be passable for maintenance vehicles, but fun enough to merit the trip from Chicago.

There are also 21 miles of bridle trails and 35 miles of cross-county and snowmobile trails, plus two manmade lakes.

Just outside the park, the 39-mile Military Ridge Trail leads to nearby Blue Mound State Park. It

was converted out of an old Chicago & Northwestern Railroad bed.

The park service says Governor Dodge's sandstone bluffs date back some 450 million years to when the area was covered by vast inland seas. After the seas retreated, wind carved into the seabed and formed the bluffs. Native Americans camped at the base of the bluffs for 8,000 years previous to the area's settlement by Europeans.

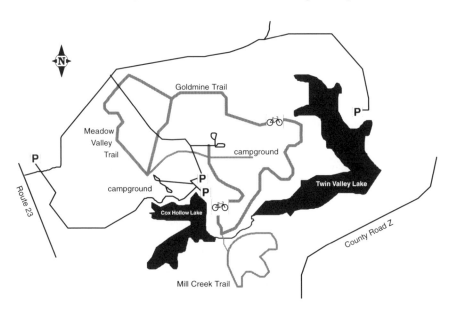

Emma Carlin
Trails

(414) 594-2135

Physical Challenge:	★★★☆
Technical Challenge:	★★☆☆
Singletrack:	60%
Doubletrack:	30%
Total Distance:	16+ miles
Distance from Loop:	95 miles
Tread:	dirt, sand

About two hours away from Chicago by car, Emma Carlin trail system in the southern unit of the Kettle Moraine State Forest is a popular destination for Illinois mountain bikers willing to roadtrip.

Carlin's got all the ingredients to make for a great day on a bike, including steep hills, acres of trees, physical and technical challenges galore and miles of dirt trails.

There is the 2.2-mile Orange Loop, the 1.6-mile Red Loop and the 5.6-mile Green Loop. All three share the same features: a lot of ups and downs, rocks, and other tough hazards.

Most of the trail corridors are wide enough for cross-country skiers but in sections they narrow, creating tight corridors that take agility. With so much breaking going on, anticipation is key to avoid dabbing or wrecking. Prepare to be both humbled and exhilirated.

In addition to hills and valleys, there are other stretches that cut through long rows of pine trees. The tread is smooth as butter in these sections.

The Wisconsin Department of Natural Resources installed water bars at Carlin in the mid-1990s as part of a comprehensive erosion control system that includess limestone screenings and resin, which reduces dust.

For crews to fill ruts -- some of which were more than a foot deep and as long as a footbal field -- certain trails were widened to permit access by maintenance vehicles. Though not as technically challenging as in the early 1990s, they're still fun for more advanced riders.

A tough 7-mile connector trail leads to nearby John Muir trail cluster. Access it about halfway around the Green Loop.

Trail passes are required by the DNR.

Call ahead for trail conditions. The system is often closed in the spring due to wet weather.

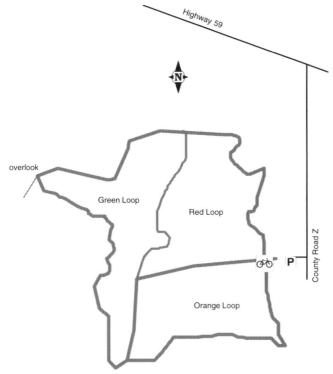

Chequamegon
National Forest
(800) 533-7454

Physical Challenge: ☆ ☆ ☆ ☆
Technical Challenge: ☆ ☆ ☆ ☆
Singletrack: 45-85 %
Doubletrack: 25-85 %
Total Distance: 300+ miles
Distance from Loop: 410 miles
Tread: dirt, gravel, sand

The Chequamegon National Forest's mountain bike system is divided into six clusters, each having 25 to 75 miles of trail and one or more trail heads. Together, the clusters offer more than 300 miles of developed trail diversions for riders of all abilities.

Located about 410 miles from Chicago, the forest is the only area listed in the *Chicago Mountain Bike Trails Guide* that takes more than a day to drive to, explore, and drive back. It's also the only one where riders are liable to see black bears and bald eagles.

The routes follow a variety of connected paths, including logging roads, snowmobile trails, fire lanes, ski trails and singletrack.

Years ago, before the trails were marked, getting lost in the 850,000-acre forest was to be expected. Now it is very easily avoided. The Chequamegon Area Mountain Bike Association (CAMBA) has detailed maps of all the trails. Pick up a copy

in any North Woods bike shop or call ahead to have them mailed. There are also reassurance markers posted to keep riders abreast of their progress.

For those who like to get off the beaten path, there are hundreds, if not thousands, of trail miles that haven't been mapped.

The Cable Cluster offers varying degrees of difficulty, from gradual doubletrack ascents to sprightly singletrack. It provides access to the famed Short & Fat Trail and the excruciatingly lengthy American Birkebeiner Trail.

The Delta Cluster is a little bit more diverse with easy dirt roads, tough singletrack and everything in between. It provides access to the North Country Recreational Trail and the White River Fishery Area with a scenic overlook above White River Valley. Its Rock Lake and Delta Hills loops are considered some of the toughest in all northern Wisconsin.

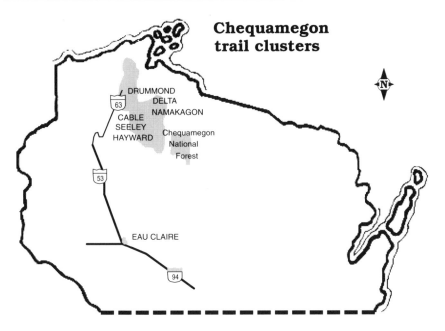

Chequamegon
trail clusters

The Namakagon Cluster offers mostly moderate riding with easy road sections and breezy single-track. It accesses paths in the Rock Lake non-motorized area and a bunch of remote national forest trails.

The Drummond Cluster has more easy road sections and moderate cross-country ski trails that connect with the Flynn Lake and Star Lake non-motorized areas.

The Seeley Cluster has difficult ski trails interspersed with moderate road sections that join the Birkebeiner Trail. It also has a stunning overlook of the Namakagon River Valley.

A great time to check out trails in the Chequamegon area is during the Chequamegon Fat Tire Festival -- the largest competitive off-road riding event in the country. Held every fall, more than 2,500 riders usually show up to engage in a weekend-long series of races and bike-related events, including an always-brutal 40-mile race.

If planning to attend, mail the application at least six months in advance. This thing is popular.

Lapham Peak

(414) 646-4421

Physical Challenge: ☆ ☆ ☆
Technical Challenge: ☆
Singletrack: 55%
Doubletrack: 25%
Total Distance: 5 miles
Distance from Loop: 120 miles
Tread: dirt, grass

The debut of a new off-road bicycle trail in the Lapham Peak
Unit of the Kettle Moraine State Forest in 1997 could impact a Chicago
biker's life in any number of ways.
A visit could entail broken chains,
exhilarating downhill thrills, curses,
sweat, bratwursts for sure, maybe
a speeding ticket or two. Who
knows? This is Wisconsin.

The trail at Lapham Peak, 30 miles
west of Milwaukee, is a lot like trails
in the Southern and Northern units
of the hallowed forest, with plenty
of steep hills on rolling moraine topography. The high point is its
namesake peak, which, at a whop-
ping 1,233 feet, is Waukesha
County's highest spot.

The trail was built as a response
to erosion and user conflicts involving bikes on a park ski trail. Laid
out on 310 acres of former farmland
acquired by the Wisconsin Department of Natural Re-
sources in 1994 and
1995, the new route
is specifically de-
signed for mountain
biking.

Thanks to volunteer
work by the local
chapter of the Wis-
consin Off-Road Bi-
cycle Association and
other users, the new
digs offers a tenth of
a mile longer ride
than what was previ-

ously available.

The trail's highest point is about 200 feet lower than the old one, but steep elevation changes are the same, some exceeding more than 130 feet.

A lot of the tread is grass, but there's plenty of doubletrack and singletrack sections. Continued use should eliminate much of their bumps, which are from its previous incarnation as a farm, a DNR spokesman said.

While there are few technical challenges, the trail does have a moderate amount of downhill turns that require steering agility and breaking prowess.

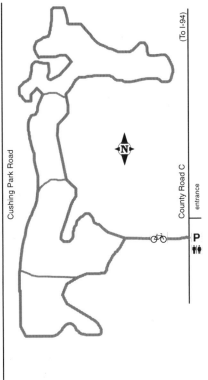

Bong
Recreation Area
(414) 878-5600

Physical Challenge: ☆

Technical Challenge: ☆

Singletrack: 10%

Doubletrack: 25%

Total Distance: 12 miles

Distance from Loop: 70 miles

Tread: grass, dirt

Bong has four color-coded mountain bike trails that are marked one-way. Adapted from 12 miles of hiking trails in the early 1990s, the bike trails run up to 8 miles, with the Orange Loop having the greatest elevation changes. Most of the loops' hills do not exceed 10 feet, though one man-made hill has a brief, 20-foot descent.

Compared to the rolling Wisconsin farmland surrounding Bong, the interior of the area is strikingly devoid of elevation changes. And there's hardly a natural landmark to be seen other than small patches of trees. Most of the trail plods through mowed grass across wide-open fields.

If the flat landscape seems a bit unusual compared to the rolling farmland surrounding the park, that's because it is. According to the state's Department of Natural Resources, Bong's history goes back to 1952, when the federal government decided that Chicago and Milwaukee needed a strategic air base to guard against invasion. Plans were put in motion to build the air base and, by 1958, land had been purchased from 59 families in Kenosha and Racine counties. Crews worked around the

clock stripping topsoil from 3,500 acres while beaurocrats decided to name the base after Maj. Richard Bong, a Wisconsin fighter ace.

In 1959, after nearly $29 million had been spent and three days before cement trucks were scheduled to surface the runway, the project was halted. Under heavy public scrutiny and with the advent of intercontinental ballistic missiles, the Defense Department decided Chicago and Milwaukee could survive without the base.

Since then, the DNR has acquired most of the land and is restoring it to its original condition. As a recreation area, Bong differs from a state park because of the activities available. Ultralights and gliders, for example, use part of what was supposed to be the runway for jets and bombers.

Are the trails crowded? Not by a long shot. Only about 500 seasonal and daily trail passes are sold each year.

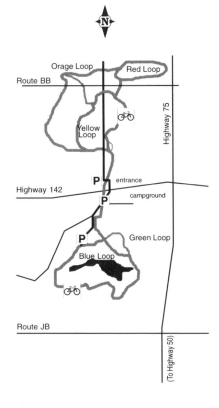

Devil's Head Resort

(800) 472-6670

Physical Challenge:	☆☆☆☆
Technical Challenge:	☆☆☆
Singletrack:	50 %
Doubletrack:	30 %
Total Distance:	25 miles
Distance from Loop:	195 miles
Tread:	dirt, grass

Devil's Head Resort, one of the Midwest's most popular ski areas, unveiled 25 miles of dirt trails in 1995 as way to generate business during non-snow months.

Adapted from walking and fitness trails, the system, if not the one of most difficult within a day's drive from Chicago, is probably the most scenic.

According to a resort spokesman, about 75 percent of the system is beginner or intermediate, and the remainder either advanced or expert. But who's kidding who? All these trails are tough. Plan on a lot of climbing and a lot of braking.

The beginner and intermediate trails start out on the fitness trail and gradually climb about halfway to the top of the resort's highest peak. While much of the routes traverse grassy hillsides away from trees, the views afforded are spectacular. With wildflowers in the foreground and the hills of south-central Wisconsin in the distance, the scenery offers plenty of reason to stop for a breather.

Advanced and expert trails here are almost exclusively uphill and require grueling climbs to make it to the top of the chairlifts, about 500 feet above the lodge. Both differ from the beginner and intermediate runs because of an endless barrage of obstacles. On a few uphill runs, rocks, blowdowns and ruts are so plentiful that they nearly obscure the trail.

For sheer thrills, there's a long descent on the west side of the resort. It cruises down a ski slope and ends up near the lodge.

Perhaps the most stunning thing about Devil's Head, even more than the views, are its plans for the future. With more than 800 acres available, the resort plans on expanding the system to more than 50 miles.

Overnight lodging and bike rentals are available. There's a bike shop in the lodge in case you forget a repair kit.

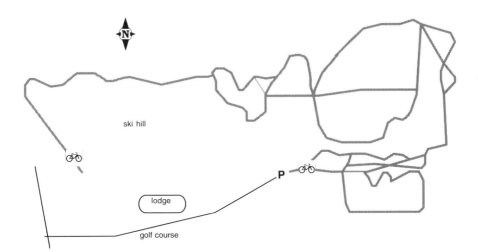

Blue Mound
State Park
(608) 437-5711

Physical Challenge: ☆☆☆
Technical Challenge: ☆
Singletrack: 10 %
Doubletrack: 25 %
Total Distance: 5 miles
Distance from Loop: 170 miles
Tread: grass, dirt, asphalt, gravel

In 1766, an English explorer described in his journal the peaks outside Blue Mound as "mountains." Bloody shame he didn't have a bike with him.

Located 25 miles west of Madison, Blue Mound State Park sports a single 5-mile bike loop over what the Wisconsin Department of Natural Resources says is the highest peak in the southern part of the state. With an elevation of 1,716 feet, the top of Blue Mound is 415 feet above the surrounding countryside.

The tread surface is mowed grass and measures up to 10 feet wide. There are a few short stretches where singletrack is developing directly down the center, but overall, it's grass.

The designated bike loop, comprising portions of the John Minix, Walnut Hollow, Ridgeview, and Pleasure Valley trails, was laid in the late 1980s. It's well marked and impossible to get lost on. The route circumvents most of the park's wooded areas and instead traverses its barren hillsides. There are virtually zero obstacles of any kind, which makes it an easy ride, except for the hills.

There are several miles of other trails in the 1,260-acre park, but they're banned to bikes.

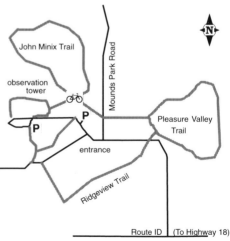

NORTHERN INDIANA

PART III

France Park

(219) 753-2928

Physical Challenge: ☆ ☆
Technical Challenge: ☆ ☆ ☆
Singletrack: 50 %
Doubletrack: 20 %
Length: 6 miles
Distance from Loop: 115 miles
Tread: dirt, grass, gravel

Taking a wrong turn on one of France Park's mountain bike trails means you sail off a 70-foot cliff into a water-filled quarry.

The trail, referred to by park employees as "the one that goes 'round the swim pond," is just one of the many interesting features in the 530-acre park. It's considered one of the best places for mountain biking in northern Indiana and annually hosts a race on the Do Indiana Offroad (DINO) mountain bike circuit.

A quick two-hour car ride from Chicago, the trails here consists of three 1-mile paths that run parallel to each other, plus another 3-mile trail that circles the park's perimeter.

The parallel trails are in a wooded section of the park's south side. There's a gutsy stream crossing before the paths converge and circle a small lake called "the fish pond." A 10-foot waterfall makes for a scenic conclusion.

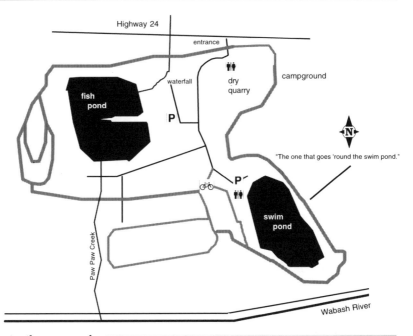

The trails are good for a smooth, fun ride through trees, but they're not half as exciting as the quarry ride. That one makes a radical ascent along a wiry dirt trail interspersed with step-like slabs of rock. Once on top of the quarry, it cruises close to the edge for a half mile, then comes down another section just as steep.

With lots of ledges, trees, dropoffs and ruts, plus the quarry just a few feet away, it's probably the most potentially perilous trail within a day's drive of Chicago.

According to a park supervisor who spoke from personal experience, people used to jump from the top of the quarry into the water, but that sort of thing is frowned on today.

The easiest way to pick up the quarry trail is next to the swim pond's beach. Enter the woods and turn left at the fork in the path and climb a hill to the quarry's top. Turning right leads to the parallel trails.

There are also some doubletrack trails in a second quarry which has a gravel bottom.

The park charges for admission and trail passes.

Bluhm Property

(219) 326-9600

Physical Challenge:

Technical Challenge:

Singletrack: 75 %

Doubletrack: 20 %

Length: 5 miles

Distance from Loop: 70 miles

Tread: dirt, grass, gravel

The Bluhm Property has a sprightly trail system that consists of two, 2-mile loops and a couple of shortcuts. It has been used for mountain biking since 1991, when Gayle and Lucille Bluhm donated the property to the LaPorte County Park Foundation, Inc.

When the Bluhms donated the land, the foundation asked county residents what should be done to upgrade it. And local mountain bikers, eager to expand riding opportunities in the area, quickly volunteered to build a trail system.

Though the trail is designed for multipurpose use, including horseback riding, cross-country skiing and hiking, it was mountain bikers who made most of the site improvements, according to a foundation spokesperson. More than 100 riders are estimated to visit each week in the summer.

Because of the dizzying number of turns, the route challenges riders' technical skills and agility. It's nothing but smooth singletrack from beginning to end, with an occasional root, stump or log. The only straightaway is a narrow, quarter-mile strip of land which connects the parking lot with the woods.

As for physical challenges, the trail is easy, with few hills more than 10 feet high. This fact can be a blessing to inexperienced riders since the left and rights are difficult enough without the added challenge of ups and downs.

The Bluhms donated the property to the nonprofit foundation, rather than the LaPorte County Parks Department, as a means of maximizing federal grant money when it's someday turned over to the county. In the interim, the foundation erected signs along the trail and built a parking lot.

The National Off-Road Bicycling Association (NORBA) has sanctioned races here for several years.

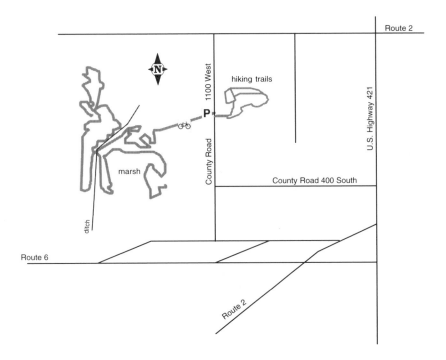

Lake Wawasee
Trail
(800) 800-6090

Physical Challenge:

Technical Challenge:

Singletrack: 85 %

Doubletrack: 10 %

Length: 4+ miles

Distance from Loop: 120 miles

Tread: dirt, grass

L ake Wawasee bike trails are jammed into a small parcel of private property just north of Syracuse. A good time to check them out are during a Do Indiana Offroad (DINO) mountain bike race, which makes a stop here once or twice a year.

Using every inch of available space, the group of fat tire enthusiasts who built the system in the early 1990s managed to squeeze in more than 4 miles of singletrack. The path they hacked out requires riders to dart around like a pinball, constantly changing direction and setting up for the next turn.

Elevation-wise, the trails tackle a couple moderate slopes. There are three directions a rider can head from the main trailhead, but all the routes eventually loop together.

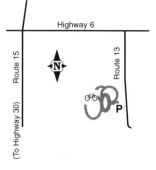

Calumet
Trail

(219) 926-7561

Physical Challenge:

Technical Challenge:

Singletrack: - %

Doubletrack: 35 %

Length: 12 miles

Distance from Loop: 50 miles

Tread: dirt, grass

Refer to map at left, top biker, for trail location.

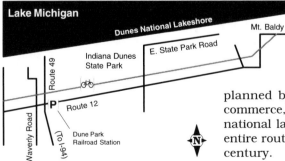

Calumet Trail was built by the Indiana Department of Natural Resources in 1976 as a scenic bicycle link between Michigan City and Indiana Dunes State Park, located on the Indiana Dunes National Lakeshore.

The trail runs beneath power lines owned by the Northern Indiana Public Service Company and comes within eyeshot of oak and maple forests, marshes and, of course, sand dunes, including soaring Mt. Baldy.

The closest trailhead to Chicago is on its west end. Pedaling east, the path is basically a long straightaway with an occasional zigzag. Most of the trail is eight feet wide, but in several sections used by four-wheel vehicles, it splits into doubletrack.

Tracks for the Chicago South Shore & South Bend Railroad run parallel to the trail.

While imperfections in the surface are minor for fat tires, the biggest obstacles are puddles. A $900,000 repair project being planned by the local chamber of commerce, county, state park and national lakeshore will replace the entire route around the turn of the century.

Imagination Glen

(219) 762-5425

Physical Challenge: ☆ ☆
Technical Challenge: ☆ ☆ ☆
Singletrack: 90 %
Doubletrack: 5 %
Length: 4+ miles
Distance from Loop: 50 miles
Tread: dirt

I magination Glen's sprightly Outback Trail is marked by hills, a couple of stream crossings, logs aplenty, and some of the sweetest singletrack a tire could caress.

The trail has been open since late 1997 when local riders hatched a plan with the City of Portage to bring mountain biking to the 256-acre park. Its name was coined through a contest with school kids after the city aquired the property in 1976. At the time, much of it was woods and former farmland "and it just sat there for a while," but funds became available in the mid-1980s to offer recreational oportunites, a park spokesman said. Today there are softball and soccer fields, a couple of archery ranges, fishing, and of course, mountain biking.

The Outback Trail avoids the ball fields by sticking to wooded areas in the park's perimeter. Much of the main 2.5-mile loop runs along Salt Creek, and another 1.5-mile section runs outside the park atop an aban-

doned railroad bed.

Building the new system wasn't a walk in the park, however. About two miles of trail had to be cleared and maintenance is a constant chore for the city and local riders.

Though there are few trail signs, the route is easily followed from the trailhead. It starts out as a gradual descent on a winding dirt path before narrowing and heading into the heart of woods. Elevation changes exceed more than 30 feet in several spots, yet perhaps the best sections are the flattest, where pristine singletrack squirrels like a dream through short grass along Salt Creek.

Other highlites include a couple of wooden bridges, a land bridge, and the stream crossings. About four feet wide, each stream is a tributary to the creek.

Eventually, more signs will be installed and the system will be expanded to virgin woods on the opposite side of the creek. To get there, a bridge will be built, pending the availability of donated materials.

Call for information on NORBA-sanctioned mountain bike races.

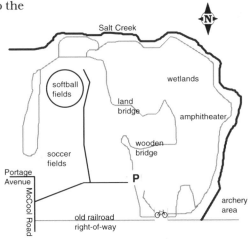

Pines Peak
Ski Area
(219) 477-5993

Physical Challenge:	☆☆☆☆
Technical Challenge:	☆☆
Singletrack:	75 %
Doubletrack:	20 %
Length:	5 miles
Distance from Loop:	65 miles
Tread:	dirt, grass, gravel

With two quarter-mile sections of trail ascending a spectacular 175 feet, Pines Peak ski hill has few rivals in Indiana for uphill challenges. But the hill's status as a mountain biking venue is uncertain as the owners deal with liability issues for both daily riding and occasional races. Call for current trail policies.

From the base, the trail leads straight up the face of the hill, zigzags near the top, then plunges down the back into the heart of the resort's 36-wooded acres. The next two miles are marked by relentless technical challenges, followed by another climb to the top. From there, it heads down the face of the hill into a sweeping 180-degree turn. The trail climbs about a quarter of the way up the hill again, but returns to the base to complete the loop.

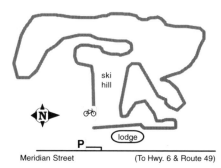

SOUTHWESTERN MICHIGAN

PART IV

Yankee Springs
State Park
(616) 795-9081

Physical Challenge: ★★★★★
Technical Challenge: ★★★★★
Singletrack: 75 %
Doubletrack: 15 %
Length: 12+
Distance from Loop: 175 miles
Tread: dirt, sand

Yankee Springs State Park is a 5,000-acre mountain bike holy land.

Located about 40 miles north of Kalamazoo, the park is not much farther from Chicago than the beloved Kettle Moraine State Forest in Wisconsin and the terrain is just as challenging.

There are nearly 30 miles of trails in Yankee Springs, 12 of which are designated for mountain biking.

The Mountain Bike Trail explores most of the northeast section, including Devil's Soup Bowl, Pines Scenic Area and Graves Hill Overlook. Because of the topographical diversity, it's nearly impossible to have a bad time here.

The place has hills. Big hills. In one part, the trail twists down the side of a steep, wooded slope, only to return to the top, head down again, return to the top and head down yet again. It's both scenic and fatiguing. The park has a lake to cool off in after a long day.

A majority of the Mountain Bike Trail is thin singletrack and made of dirt. Even in areas where the corridor widens out a bit, it is constantly passing through trees and going around bogs, marshes, lakes and streams. Some of it is sandy, but overall, it's hard and fast. Trail markers are posted along the way and detailed maps are available at park headquarters.

The park reportedly draws mountain bike visitors from as far away as the East Coast. Most out-of-towners camp at rustic Deep Lake Campground, where the trailhead is just a few yards away. For bikers that like to camp, this place may be unbeatable in the southern Great Lakes region.

The park's history dates back to when it was prime hunting grounds for Algonquin Indians, led in the 18th century by Chief Noonday. It's appeal for hunters still exists, so be careful not to visit during fall deer season.

Call in advance for trail conditions. Trail passes are required.

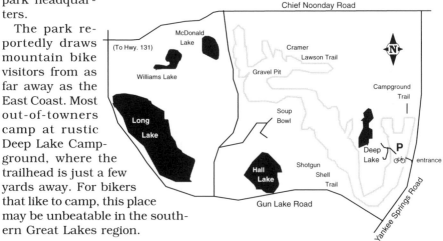

Ft. Custer
State Park
(616) 731-4200

Physical Challenge: ☆☆☆
Technical Challenge: ☆☆☆
Singletrack: 70 %
Doubletrack: 20 %
Length: 7 miles
Distance from Loop: 157 miles
Tread: dirt, sand

Ft. Custer Recreation Area is the second of two killer mountain bike areas near Kalamazoo.

Like Yankee Springs State Park 50 miles to the northeast, it has miles of wooded trails that traverse hills, ravines, bogs and streams, or just about every challenge a Midwest biker could realistically hope for.

The designated mountain bike trail, known as the Red Loop, passes a variety of unusual landscape features with names like "Rocks and Roots," "Gravel Pit," "Crazy Beaver," and "Freeway." The Southwest Chapter of the Michigan Mountain Bike Association, which helps maintain the trail, named each section in the early 1990s.

The route climbs and descends small hills and weaves through timber like a maze. By far, the most unusual part is "The Trenches," where it runs through trenches dug by soldiers training for World War I, when the park was known as Ft. Custer Military Training Center. (In

1969, about a third of the training center's 11,000 acres were turned over to the DNR for recreational use.) Another hot spot is "No Fear Chute," which is a steep descent with a giant mogul midway down. Bonus points are awarded for catching air, landing safely, and finessing into turn-laden "Amusement Park." "Granny's Garden" is the most technical section, and so named because of the granny gear needed to avoid putting a foot down.

Two more loops, maintained exclusively by the state's Department of Natural Resources, circle Jackson Hole, Whitford and Lawler lakes. They're not quite as hot as the Red Loop but are still challenging as they twist through tall grasses and fertile fields. They all connect with each other and make for miles of riding. There are

also a couple miles of Jeep trails in the park. Trail markers keep riders going in the correct direction.

Because hunting is allowed in the park much of the year, check with the ranger's office to see if it's safe to ride. The office will also answer questions on trail conditions.

A trail pass is required to ride.

NEW, EXPANDED
& MISCELLANEOUS
TRAILS

PART V

McDowell Grove
Forest Preserve

(630) 933-7200

Physical Challenge: ☆
Technical Challenge: ☆
Singletrack: 40 %
Doubletrack: 30 %
Length: 5 miles
Distance from Loop: 27 miles
Tread: grass, dirt

Riding through the trail system at McDowell Grove near Naperville, it's easy to see why the U.S. Army used it during World War II as a top-secret radar installation. Its thick forests must have been ideal for obscuring the Army's development of radar technology, and its relative seclusion along the West Branch of the DuPage River must have made it difficult for spies or neighbors to know what was going on.

The multi-loop trail system on site today is mostly grass with stretches of singletrack running down the center. It's a nice change from the crushed rock at most DuPage County trails and lends to the rustic scenery.

The 416-acre preserve was acquired by the U.S. Defense Department in the early 1940s. Then called Camp McDowell, the site was used to develop radar technology and, by war's end, reportedly housed half of the world's equipment. It was later transferred to the county for open space purposes.

None of the military complex remains today except for some gravelly old roads, an old bridge and a pervading sense of solitude.

The preserve in the late 1990s served as a flashpoint among county forest preserve officials, some of whom wanted to turn it onto two separate preserves to accommodate a road project. The idea was shot down and the road diverted, leaving the preserve largely intact.

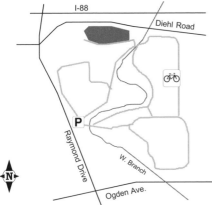

Jubilee College
State Park

(309) 446-3758

Physical Challenge:	☆☆☆
Technical Challenge:	☆☆☆
Singletrack:	75 %
Doubletrack:	15 %
Length:	27+ miles
Distance from Loop:	155 miles
Tread:	dirt

Jubilee College State Park is host to what are widely regarded as the best off-road bicycle trails in central Illinois.

The park's Southern Tier trail system has a half-dozen loops and subloops good for 15 miles of generally smooth riding. The Northern Tier has at least 12 more, with steep gullies, log bridges and other hazards that are prevalent without being overly challenging.

Elevation changes in the park max out at about 75 feet, with trails mimicking a roller coaster as they pass through the Illinois River Valley's many wooded hills, ravines and rocky outcroppings.

According to park officials, the system developed in the 1970s, long after the state acquired the land from the defunct Jubilee College, a pioneer-era school.

Rarely crowded except for sanctioned races, the system continues to expand thanks to accommodating park management and the diligence of local riders.

Due to its central Illinois location, the riding season starts in early spring and often lasts well into the fall.

Camping is available in a sparse but convenient campground. No reservations are necessary.

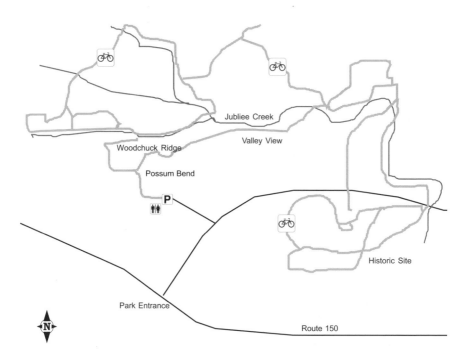

Catlin Park

(815) 434-0518

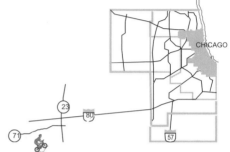

Physical Challenge: ★★★
Technical Challenge: ★★★
Singletrack: 65 %
Doubletrack: 10 %
Length: 13 miles
Distance from Loop: 90 miles
Tread: dirt, gravel

Located in the shadows of one of Illinois' most scenic waterways, Catlin Park of LaSalle County revels in its own obscurity. No crowds, no traffic and, most of all, no bicycle prohibitions.

Catlin is near a bluff-lined stretch of the Illinois River near Starved Rock State Park, 90 miles southwest of Chicago. Starved Rock would be a better bicycling venue than Catlin, but due to bicycling restrictions there, Catlin is the next best option.

Its 13-mile trail system meanders up and down hills, through streams and across wide expanses of prairie. Required effort varies from the benign White Tail Run Trail to the challenging Ooooooh Heck Hill.

The park's 330 acres are divided into east and west sections, each containing about a half-dozen individual trails. Maps are available at the end of the gravel road leading to the main parking area between the two sections.

Because the park is several miles from the river, there's none of the rugged sandstone bluffs and stream-fed canyons that make Starved Rock a geological wonderland. The most significant natural formations here are steep, 50-foot ravines that take a lot of handling to avoid hangups. In the west section, Ooooooh Heck Hill makes a switchback descent into a ravine, passes through Brown Creek, then ascends a set of switchbacks on the other side.

In the east section, Wet-Foot Trail meanders along the bottom of a ravine, leapfrogging back and forth across a creek every 25 yards.

Easier trails run throughout the park, such as Prairie Trail, which runs adjacent to tall grasses, and others that border corn and soybean fields.

Most of the trails are at least eight feet wide, but there are several wooded areas where the corridor narrows into thin singletrack amid towering oaks and hickories. Other sections are doubletrack and, de-

spite their use by horses, they're in excellent shape.

The main draw for the park, other than its trail system, is its wildlife. Deer are everywhere, and it's not uncommon to spot pheasants, turkeys and red-tailed hawks.

Cross-country skiing also used to be encouraged in the park, but due to fluctuating weather and a drop-off in visitors, the park closes for the season at the end of October.

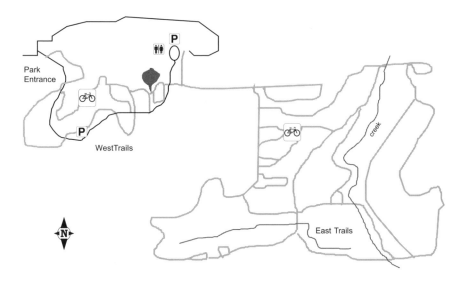

Crystal Ridge
Ski Hill

(414) 529-7676

MILWAUKEE

CHICAGO

Physical Challenge: ★★★★
Technical Challenge: ★★★
Singletrack: 70 %
Doubletrack: 20 %
Length: 3 miles
Distance from Loop: 85 miles
Tread: dirt, gravel

With layers of earth piled high above the southern Wisconsin countryside, Crystal Ridge Ski Hill resembles a giant wedding cake. Appropriately enough, the hill and mountain bikes seem like a perfect match.

Located about 80 miles north of Chicago in the Milwaukee suburb of Franklin, Crystal Ridge is owned by Milwaukee County and used as a ski hill during the winter. In summer, it's opened to bikes for special events--mostly time trials that are

held each week. Every 30 seconds, a pair of riders set out on a marked loop that tackles the hills best features. The only requirement is a modest entry fee and membership in the statewide mountain biking association.

The course changes from week to week but it usually starts near a ski lodge located about midway up the hill. It climbs a short access road toward the summit before skipping onto a ski run and descending a steep series of switchbacks to the base.

Next is an old bridal path along Root River, a stretch of singletrack through woods, and a final, long climb back up to the lodge. Total length is about three miles. Most trials go for three to five laps and most competitors finish in 20 to 30 minutes.

The hill has a 240-foot elevation change, making it one of the most strenuous, and fast,

in the area.

The site is also an active landfill where local waste haulers make regular deposits. The activity is on the backside and doesn't affect the trails on the front.

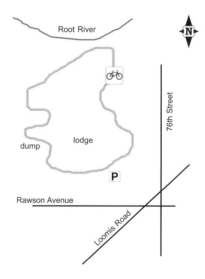

Green Valley
Forest Preserve

(630) 933-7200

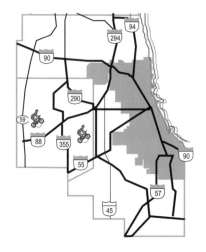

Physical Challenge: ☆
Technical Challenge: ☆
Singletrack: 10 %
Doubletrack: 10 %
Length: 16 miles
Distance from Loop: 35 miles
Tread: crushed rock

With five separate loops rang-
ing from one to three miles,
the trail system at Greene Valley
is the third longest in the DuPage
County forest preserve system.
And by virtue of its location along
the east branch of the DuPage
River, it's hillier than all but the
trails at nearby Waterfall Glen
preserve.

The system passes through oak
savannas, prairies and, north of
79th Street, several fields of wildflowers. Though expansive, the trails are
manicured and graded for easy access, making it ideal for beginners
but rather mundane for riders with
intermediate skills.

The preseve's largest element is
a waste dump that rises nearly
100 feet above the river. The
dump, capped with grass
and filled with more than 1
million cubic yards of garbage, is off-limits to bikes.

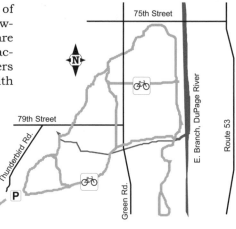

Fullersburg Woods
Forest Preserve

(630) 850-8110

Physical Challenge:	☆
Technical Challenge:	☆
Singletrack:	0 %
Doubletrack:	10 %
Length:	5 miles
Distance from Loop:	35 miles
Tread:	crushed rock

SEE MAP AT LEFT, RIGHT BIKER, FOR TRAIL LOCATION

Opened to the public way back in 1920, Fullersburg Wood's 222 acres have several small, looped trails good for exertion-free riding.

The easiest is the aptly-named Multipurpose Trail, which is also the preserve's longest. Somewhat harder is the Interpretive Trail, which leads visitors through lowland woods and prairie, most of it following Salt Creek along the water's edge. And the Wildflower Trail, also moderately easy, travels a short distance through woods and restored prairie.

There's also a short trail to Graue Mill, a century-old National Historic Landmark, and another to the 150-year-old house of Benjamin Fuller, who helped found the suburb of Oak Brook and for whom the preserve is named.

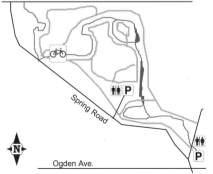

Danada and Herrick Lake
Forest Preserves
(630) 933-7200

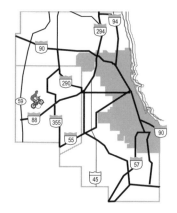

Physical Challenge:	☆
Technical Challenge:	☆
Singletrack:	5 %
Doubletrack:	15 %
Length:	8+ miles
Distance from Loop:	30 miles
Tread:	crushed rock

It's been nearly 40 years since Wheaton's Lucky Debonair won the Kentucky Derby, but visiting the trail at the thoroughbred's former home at Danada Forest Preserve, it might as well have been yesterday. Stables, a practice track and other tools of the horse racing trade are still in place.

Danada, along with its sister preserve, Herrick Lake, are a unique daily double on the Chicago-area off-road bicycling circuit. Visitors can tour both locations without ever leaving the same trail. There's more than eight miles of riding available and it's virtually the same rolling landscape that Lucky Debonair viewed while training for what would be the third fastest race in Derby history.

The two preserves are located side by side, each the product of county land acquisitions from the 1920s through the 1980s. They're con-nected by the eight-mile Regional Trail, a crushed rock path that makes a seamless transition from one preserve to the other.

The bulk of the mileage is in 760-acre Herrick Lake preserve. Named for early DuPage homesteader Ira Herrick, the preserve sports the Regional Trail plus the Meadowlark, Green Heron and Bluebird trails. Each loop provides a serene ride through a mix of stately oaks, wet-lands and tall prairie. Due to years of habitat improvement projects, such as an ongoing restoration of Herrick's South Woods, the only remnants of its homestead days is an occasional weathered fence row. A separate loop circles the preserve's 21-acre lake.

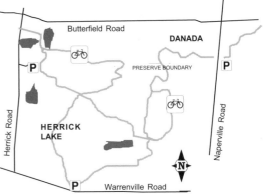

There's no marker where the Regional Trail passes out of Herrick Lake and into the 783-acre Danada preserve. The only indicators are an old racing starting gate and a half-mile oval maintained by a local equestrian group.

In addition to the Regional Trail, Danada has a couple sections of grassy doubletrack that are opened to bikes. The routes meander past Rice Lake and through open prairie before converging and entering a tunnel below Naperville Road. After emerging on the other side of the road, the trail detours into Parson's Grove, where a thin nature trail has about a mile of additional riding.

With easy turns, smooth surfaces and maximum elevation changes of 15 feet, the preserves are suitable for beginner to intermediate riders.

Wilmot Mountain
Bike Park
(262) 862-2301

Physical Challenge: ★★★ ★
Technical Challenge: ★★ ★
Singletrack: 35 %
Doubletrack: 35 %
Length: 5+ miles
Distance from Loop: 60 miles
Tread: dirt, gravel, grass

The closest off-road biking location to Chicago with chair lifts adapted for bikes, Wilmot ski resort-turned-bike park is a unique, relatively new venue that's privately owned but accessible to the public. Opened in 1999, the trail system hosts one of the area's only sanctioned bike races involving downhill and slalom events, each on the face of the hill. Cross-country events travel far into the property's 450 acres, including the summit and a stretch along the Fox River. The summit--a stone's throw from the Illinois state line-- rises to about 970 feet above sea level; 250 feet higher than the parking lot.

About one third of the route consists of doubletrack, another third is grass, and the remainder is singletrack. Highlights include a series of wooded switchbacks to the top, a gravelpit, and a fast drop from the top down to the lodge.

The resort originally opened in 1938. Its transition from skiing to a year-round resort was purely demand-driven, according to its designers, who recruited more than two dozen volunteers from several area bike organizations to complete the trail project. Some existing foot paths and game trails were used, also some service roads, while others were built from scratch.

Trail passes are available for a small fee and include access to a lift that's been modified to carry bikes. Many vistors prefer to grunt the way to the top.

Though portions of the trail can be tough, novice riders shouldn't be too intimidated. Difficulty levels are marked and most tough sections can be easily walked or avoided.

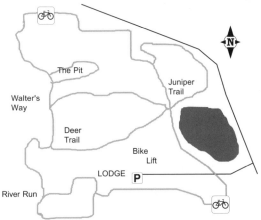

Pratt's Wayne Woods
Forest Preserve
(630) 933-7200

Physical Challenge: ☆
Technical Challenge: ☆
Singletrack: 0 %
Doubletrack: 0 %
Length: 12 miles
Distance from Loop: 33 miles
Tread: crushed rock

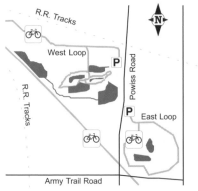

Pratt's Wayne Woods is a flat, easy ride through woods, open fields and around flooded quarries.

Before it became a preserve, the Morton Salt company mined the land for salt and sand. Today, the quarries are flooded, providing for the trail's most unique stretch: a narrow isthmus. The route's lowlight is a required detour onto the Elgin branch of the Illinois Prairie Path to make a complete loop.

The preserve is named after former township supervisor George Pratt, who spearheaded the acquisition of the preserve into the suburb of Wayne in the 1960s. With 3,300 acres, it's today the largest forest preserve in DuPage County.

Much of the preserve is prairie with long, sweeping vistas and, on occasion, strong winds.

Buffalo Creek
Forest Preserve
(847) 367-6640

Physical Challenge: ☆
Technical Challenge: ☆
Singletrack: 0 %
Doubletrack: 0 %
Length: 4+ miles
Distance from Loop: 27 miles
Tread: crushed rock

SEE MAP AT LEFT, TOP BIKER, FOR TRAIL LOCATION

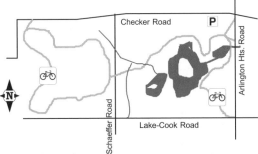

Buffalo Creek's bike trail is one of the shortest in Lake County. It was created around an enormous flood retention system that looks a lot like natural habitat. Mandmade lakes and marshes pass for the real thing; the give-away is a gigantic concrete dam that keeps tens of thousands of area homes from flooding.

The trail gives a good view of the whole system as it travels the property. Starting from the preserve's sole parking lot, the trail makes a mild descent before skirting along some marshes and gingerly heading west past the main reservoir.

The west portion of the preserve, across Schaeffer Road, was restored from farmland to native prairie in the early 1990s. The trail makes a flat loop around the prairie, crosses two bridges, then heads back to the wetland area.

The dam is near the east trailhead. When the water level exceeds 15 feet, water spills over the top of the dam into Buffalo Creek.

Blackwell
Forest Preserve
(630) 933-7200

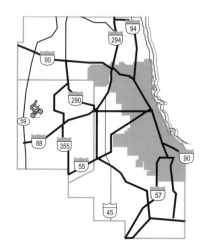

Physical Challenge: ☆
Technical Challenge: ☆
Singletrack: 0 %
Doubletrack: 0 %
Length: 8 miles
Distance from Loop: 37 miles
Tread: crushed rock

B lackwell's eight miles of trail wind around marshes and prairies that, though nice to look at, are best known for producing the skeleton of a wooly mammoth in 1977.

The mammoth was discovered some 10,000 years after it died, when conservation crews were working on the restoration of McKee Marsh. The trail passes within a stone's throw of the exact location. To see the skeleton first-hand, visit nearby Fullersburg Woods.

Elsewehere on the trail, small hills provide brief, long-distance glimpses of the preserve's 1,300 acres. The trail moves in and out of trees as it takes a leisurely route. Ideal for beginners, it may seem monotonous for riders seeking a workout.

The highest point in the preserve is Mt. Hoy, about 75 above the surrounding countryside. A former garbage dump, it isn't a part of the trail system.

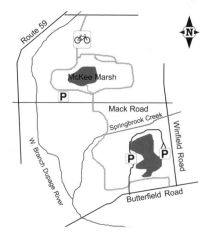

More trails...

Cook County

Thorn Creek
Length: 9+ miles
Surface: asphalt, dirt
Location: Lansing, Park Forest
Information:
Cook County Forest Preserves
536 N. Harlem Ave.
River Forest, IL 60305
(708) 366-9420

Tinley Creek
Length: 13+ miles
Surface: asphalt, dirt
Location: Midlothian, Flossmoor
Information:
Cook County Forest Preserves
536 N. Harlem Ave.
River Forest, IL 60305
(708) 366-9420

Lake County

Lakewood Forest Preserve
Length: 5+ miles
Surface: dirt, crushed rock
Location: Wauconda
Information:
Lake County Forest Preserves
2000 N. Milwaukee Ave.
Libertyville, IL 60048
(847) 367-6640

Daniel Wright Woods
Length: 5+ miles
Surface: crushed rock, dirt
Location: Vernon Hills, Lake Forest
Information:
Lake County Forest Preserves
2000 N. Milwaukee Ave.
Libertyville, IL 60048
(847) 367-6640

Green Belt Forest Preserve
Length: 8.5 miles
Surface: crushed rock
Location: North Chicago
Information:
Lake County Forest Preserves
2000 N. Milwaukee Ave.
Libertyville, IL 60048
(847) 367-6640

Lyons Woods
Length: 3 miles
Surface: crushed rock
Location: Waukegan
Information:
Lake County Forest Preserves
2000 N. Milwaukee Ave.
Libertyville, IL 60048
(847) 367-6640

Rules of the Trail

Ride on open trails only
Respect trail and road closures (ask if not sure); avoid possible trespass on private land; obtain permits and authorization as may be required. Federal and State wilderness areas are closed to cycling.

Leave no trace
Be sensitive to dirt beneath you. Even on open trails, you should not ride where you will leave evidence of your passing, such as certain soils shortly after a rain. Observe the different types of soils and trail construction; practice low-impact cycling. This also means staying on the trail and not creating any new ones. Be sure to pack out as least as much as you pack in.

Control your bicycle
Inattention for even a second can cause disaster. Excessive speed maims and threatens people; there is no excuse for it!

Always yield the trail
Make known your approach well in advance. A friendly greeting is considerate and works well; startling someone may cause loss of trail access. Show your respect when passing others by slowing to a walk or even stopping. Anticipate that other trail users may be around corners, or in blind spots.

Never spook animals
All animals are startled by an unannounced approach, a sudden movement, or a loud noise. This can be dangerous for you, for others, and for the animals. Give animals extra room and time to adjust to you. In passing, use special care and follow the directions of horseback riders (ask if uncertain). Running cattle and disturbing wild animals is a serious offense. Leave gates as you found them, or as marked.

Plan ahead
Know your equipment, and the area in which you are riding - and prepare accordingly. Be self sufficient at all times. Wear a helmet, keep your bike in good condition, and carry necessary supplies for changes in weather or other conditions. A well executed trip is a satisfaction to you and not a burden or offense to others.

ORDER FORM

Send ___ copies of the "Chicago Mountain Bike Trails Guide" to the below address:

Name   _____

Address   _____

           _____

City   _____ State _____

ZIP   _____

_____books @ $13.95   =_____

Illinois residents
add 8.75% sales tax
($1.22 per book)

                               =_____

Shipping and handling is free
for orders that include this
page. Add $2 for deliveries
outside the United States.   =_____

TOTAL   =_____

Send a check for the total amount to:

BLT Books
P.O. Box 25094, Chicago, IL 60625

Email: orders@bltbooks.com

Or order through our web site at:

www.bltbooks.com

P.L. Strazz logged more than 8,000 miles in researching off-road bicycle trails for *Chicago Mountain Bike Trails Guide* and other outdoor publications. His recent book *Surfing the Great Lakes* is among the country's bestselling surfing titles. He toils in obscurity in the Lincoln Square neighborhood of Chicago.